FLORENCE AND TUSCANY TRAVEL GUIDE
2024-2025

Meandering Through Medieval Alleyways With Map And Images, Eating local Foods,Also Admiring Renaissance Masterpieces,Summer Festival in Lucca.

Detra R. Cutler

Disclaimer:
The information provided in this guide is based on research and personal experiences as of the publication date. While every effort has been made to ensure the accuracy and completeness of the content, the author and publisher assume no responsibility for any errors, omissions, or changes in conditions that may affect the accuracy of the information. Visitors are encouraged to check current conditions and regulations before traveling.

Trademarks: All trademarks, service marks, product names, and logos appearing in this book are the property of their respective owners. Use of them does not imply any affiliation with or endorsement by them.

Table of Contents

Chapter 1. Overview   **6**

Greetings from Tuscany and Florence   6

A few quick information and travel advice.   9

Travel Advice for Tuscany and Florence   10

Chapter 2. How to Go to Tuscany   **13**

Options for Transportation   13

Handling the Tuscany Region and Florence   21

Chapter 4. Seeing the Tuscan region   **32**

History and Highlights of Siena.   32

Leaning Tower of Pisa and Beyond.   35

Lucca: Historic Walls and Uptown Elegance   37

San Gimignano, known as the Tower Town   39

Chianti Area: Wine and Rural Landscape   40

Chapter 5. Historical Sites   **43**

Ancient Roman Amphitheater at Fiesole: Immaculate Ruins   43

masterworks from the Renaissance   49

Chapter 6. Culture and Art   **51**

Galleries and Museums   51

Celebrations & Occasions   56

Chapter 7. Culinary pleasures   **64**

typical food from Tuscany   64

Top Dining Establishments   66

marketplaces for food and specialty stores   70

Chapter 8. Best Places to Stay   **75**

opulent resorts and hotels   75

Cost-effective Substitutes   77

Chapter 9.Perfect Itineraries   **80**

Three-Day Schedule for Florence 80

Seven-Day Road Trip Through Tuscany 7-Day Road Trip Schedule 84

A Family-Friendly Tuscany & Florence Itinerary 88

Chapter 10. Activities **93**

Outdoor Recreation and Natural Areas 93

Purchasing and Keeping Assortments 103

Entertainment & Nightlife 105

Chapter 11. useful knowledge **108**

Safety & Health 108

Conclusion 111

Chapter 1. Overview

Greetings from Tuscany and Florence

Greetings from the heart of Italy, where every town, slope, and winery narrates a story spanning generations. This book is your passport to exploring the hidden gems of Tuscany and Florence, two destinations that have long enthralled tourists. Regardless of your level of experience traveling to Italy, I'm excited to go on this incredible journey with you.

I was astounded by Florence's beauty and history when I first visited. There seemed to be a lively, old-world vibe about the city. The iconic Ponte Vecchio emerged as I strolled down the Arno River, its golden hues glistening in the sunlight. It felt like you were entering a different era when artisans created their goods and traders traded goods and stories.

I arrived in Tuscany's serene sceneries via my travels. The charming Piazza del Campo in Siena captivated me the most about this small town. For me, witnessing the centuries-old horse race known as the Palio was a wonderful experience. The sound of hooves on ancient stone and a boisterous crowd encircling me gave me the impression that I had traveled to a different era.

I climbed the centuries-old towers of San Gimignano, each step offering an even more breathtaking view than the last. Memories are evoked by the flavor of warm bread dipped in freshly squeezed olive oil and the scent of cypress trees in the early morning.

I am appreciative of you, my reader. It is an honor that I did not take lightly to select this guide above the many others that are accessible. I really appreciate your trust in this book, and I promise to provide you with an educational and motivating read. This book is the culmination of many hours of research, investigation, and a profound affection for this special location.

These pages are chock-full of my observations and experiences because I want to give you more than just information and recommendations—I want to tell you a story that will take you right into the heart of Florence and Tuscany. Every area, from bustling city squares to serene rural hideaways, is created to allow you to have your own unique experiences.

The voyage commences

More than just travel locations, Florence and Tuscany offer unique experiences. You will be astounded by the Duomo's grandeur in Florence, with its beautiful marble façade—a masterpiece of human ingenuity. There is an enormous collection of masterworks at the Uffizi Gallery, many of which portray different historical eras.

Strolling around the streets, you'll find trattorias luring you inside with the aroma of fresh herbs and garlic, as well as charming cafés offering the best coffee on earth. Every corner of the city holds a new delight, a diamond that is just waiting to be found.

The Tuscan countryside is made up of rolling hills that are dotted with olive and grape gardens. I tasted wines in the Chianti region that celebrated history and care with every sip, and spoke of the place from whence they came. With their ancient walls and winding pathways, medieval cities like Volterra and Monteriggioni offer a glimpse into a world where history is still being lived.

The famous Leaning Tower in Pisa is a monument to the ingenuity and tenacity of people. It feels almost surreal to ascend its spiral staircase and take in the city's views. In the meantime, Florence's creative past never ceases to amaze, with new findings being made in every museum and cathedral.

I sincerely hope you get the same sense of wonder and delight from using this guide that I did. Spend some time getting to know the locals, enjoying their cuisine, and engaging with them as they inhabit this breathtaking area. Let this book be your friend; it offers genuine inspiration and useful advice.

Once again, I appreciate you choosing this book. I hope you have an incredible time and create many priceless memories on your travels. Enjoy your travels!

A few quick information and travel advice.

Fast facts about Tuscany and Florence.

Location: The Tyrrhenian Sea lies to the west of Central Italy, bounded by Liguria, Emilia-Romagna, Umbria, and Lazio.
Florence is the capital (Firenze).
It is spoken in Italian. English is widely understood in popular tourist locations.
The Euro (€) is the unit of currency.

There are about 3.7 million people living in Tuscany, with approximately 380,000 of them living in Florence.
Mediterranean weather characterizes the area, with warm summers and mild winters. The climate is gentler by the coast than it is inland.

Time Zone: Summer is CEST, winter is CET.

Pisa Galileo Galilei (PSA) and Florence Peretola (FLR) are the two main airports.

The Historic Center of Florence, Piazza del Duomo in Pisa, Val d'Orcia, and other locations are recognized as UNESCO World Heritage Sites.

Travel Advice for Tuscany and Florence

Ideal time to go

- The best seasons are spring (April to June) and fall (September to October) when there are fewer people and lovely weather. Winters are quieter and colder, while summers can be hot and crowded.

Navigating

- Florence's downtown area is walkable. Consider taking a public bus or tram for longer trips. Steer clear of unapproved driving in restricted traffic zones, or ZTLs.

- **Tuscany**: Hiring a car is the best method to see the little towns and rural areas. Buses and trains connect the major cities.

Accommodation

- Florence offers both exquisite bed and breakfasts and opulent hotels. If you want easy access to the city's attractions, think about booking a room close to it.

- Agriturismos (farm stays), boutique hotels, and holiday homes are available in Tuscany. It's best to make reservations in advance, especially during busy times.

Eating

- Savor regional specialties like pappa al pomodoro (tomato bread soup), ribollita (Tuscan soup), and bistecca alla Fiorentina (Florentine steak).

- Don't overlook the wine! Chianti, Brunello di Montalcino, and Vino Nobile di Montepulciano are among the wines of Tuscany that are well-known.

Cultural Courtesies

- **Salutations**: A peck on each cheek or a firm handshake.

- **Eating**: leisurely dinners are favored by Italians. Enjoy the occasion and don't rush it. Tipping is not necessary, but it is traditional to round up the bill.

- **Dress Code**: Please wear modest clothing when entering churches or other places of worship.

Seeing

- **Florence**: Purchase tickets in advance to avoid long lines at popular attractions like the Accademia and the Uffizi Gallery. Venture past the main draws to uncover undiscovered gems.

- **Tuscany**: Take your time discovering the little villages and towns. Life moves at a slower pace, and every place has a certain allure.

Security

- Tuscany and Florence are very safe. Pickpockets should be avoided in crowded areas. Be aware of your surroundings and safeguard your possessions.

Words

- Acquiring a basic vocabulary of Italian terms could be beneficial. The effort is appreciated by the locals, which could enhance your experience.

Purchasing

- Florence is renowned for its fine fashion, leather goods, and jewelry made of gold. Shop at local markets like San Lorenzo for unique finds.

- **Tuscany**: Look for wine, olive oil, and artisan ceramics. Weekly markets are held in many areas where you can buy locally-grown produce.

You'll be ready to make the most of your trip to Florence and Tuscany with this quick information and advice. Savor every moment of your voyage!

Chapter 2. How to Go to Tuscany

Options for Transportation

Travel by train via Tuscany and Florence.

With its stunning scenery and convenient access to many of the region's top sites, train travel is one of the most economical and enjoyable ways to see Florence and Tuscany.

Railroad Stations in Florence

Novella Santa Maria (SMN):

- **Location**: The historic core of Florence, right in the middle of the city.

- **Amenities**: Contemporary shops, eateries, ticket offices, and baggage storage.

- **Connections**: Offers regional trains to other regions of Tuscany in addition to high-speed trains (Frecciarossa, Frecciargento) to major cities including Rome, Milan, and Venice.

Campo Di Marte:

- **Location**: Mostly serving long-distance and regional trains, northeast of the city center.

- **Facilities**: Not as large as SMN, but nevertheless equipped with standard features including restrooms, ticket machines, and a waiting area.

- **Connections**: It's easy to get to nearby regional destinations and sports events because it's next to Florence's main stadium.

Rifredi:

- **Location**: Mostly catering to regional traffic, this location is in Florence's northwest.

- **amenities**: A small waiting area and ticket machines are among the basic amenities.

- **Connections**: Crucial for regional and commuter transportation in Tuscany.

Important Stations for the Tuscany Train

Pisa Centrale:

- **Location**: One of the city's primary attractions is Central Pisa.

- Retailers, cafes, luggage storage, and ticket counters are among the amenities.

- **Connections**: Trains to Florence, Lucca, and the coast run frequently.

Siena

- **Location**: A little outside of the city center, with buses that can take you into the city.

- **Amenities**: Common areas with restrooms, ticket machines, and waiting areas.

- Direct trains to Florence and connections to other Tuscan cities are available as modes of transportation.

Lucca:

- Ideally situated next to the city walls, providing quick access to the historic district.

- **Amenities**: Simple offerings like a tiny café and ticket machines.

- **Transportation**: Florence, Pisa, and Viareggio are all connected by regular trains.

The price of a train ticket

High-speed rail systems (Frecciargento, Frecciarossa):

- **From Florence to Rome**: from €20 to €50, based on the class and time of booking.

- **From Florence to Milan**: Between €30 and €70 from Florence to Milan.

Regional railroads:

- **Pisa to Florence**: around €8–€12.

- **From Florence to Siena**: around €10–€15.

- **Lucca to Florence**: around €7–€10.

How to Travel for Less on the Train:

- To get a discount, buy your tickets online in advance.

- Take into account regional passes, which offer unlimited travel on regional trains across Tuscany.

A convenient, scenic, and often inexpensive way to experience the natural beauty and rich history of Florence and Tuscany is by train.

Bus Service in Tuscany and Florence

Buses are an excellent means of transit in Florence and throughout Tuscany, providing residents and visitors with a stable and affordable option. The extensive bus network connects major cities, towns, and even remote villages, making traveling without a car easier.

Florence

Located near the Santa Maria Novella train station on Piazza della Stazione is Florence's main bus terminal. There is a lot going on at this important hub, as buses arrive and depart often. An easy way to get around the city is the local bus service, which is run by the ATAF (Azienda Trasporti Area Fiorentina). Buses are modern and air-conditioned, making the ride enjoyable.

Purchasing a single ticket in advance from kiosks or vending machines will cost you approximately €1.50. For €2.50, tickets can also be bought on board. There can be an infinite number of transfers during the 90-minute validity period of these tickets.

Tuscany

The main bus company in Tuscany, Tiemme, links Florence with nearby cities such as Arezzo, Pisa, and Siena. These buses travel across the breathtaking Tuscan countryside in comfort and with good maintenance.

- **Siena**: Piazza Gramsci, the main bus stop, is conveniently situated and provides quick access to the historic city center.

- **Pisa**: Passengers can easily switch between trains thanks to the bus terminal's proximity to the Pisa Centrale rail station.

- **Arezzo**: The bus station is located close to the city center and other important sights on Via Guido Monaco.

Regional bus tickets range in price based on the distance traveled. For instance, a trip from Florence to Pisa typically costs about €9.00, whereas a ticket from Florence to Siena typically costs about €7.80. You can buy tickets online, at authorized dealers, and at bus terminals.

Useful Advice

- **Validating Tickets**: Don't forget to insert your ticket into the validation machine as soon as you're on board. Penalties could be imposed for failure to comply.

- **schedules**: Bus terminals and websites both have timetables. It is advised that you confirm the timetable ahead of time, especially for local travel, as some lines can operate with less service on weekends and holidays.

- **Comfort**: Regional buses offer a more relaxed trip with comfy seats and lots of luggage space, but city buses may be crowded during rush hours.

In Florence and Tuscany, traveling by bus is an easy and enjoyable way to see the breathtaking scenery and historic charm of the region.

Rent a car in Tuscany and Florence.

You may travel around Florence and Tuscany at your own pace while admiring the breathtaking scenery and exploring off-the-beaten-path locations if you rent a car. The majority of car rental companies have convenient locations at main rail terminals, city centers, and Florence Peretola and Pisa airports (FLR and PSA).

It is straightforward to pick up your vehicle from Florence Peretola Airport (FLR) car rental offices, which are often situated in the arrivals hall or adjacent to the terminal building. Similar to this, Pisa Galileo Galilei Airport (PSA) has rental shops inside the terminal, making it easy to transfer from the air to the ground.

The type of vehicle, length of rental, and optional extras (such as GPS navigation and insurance) all affect how much it costs to rent a car in Florence and Tuscany. Small automobiles usually cost between €30 and €50 per day to hire, but larger cars or more expensive models might cost as much as €80 to €100. Make your reservations early in advance to guarantee the best deals and availability, especially during the busiest travel seasons.

In Florence, tram

For those who choose to venture outside the historical area of the city, Florence's tram system offers an easy and quick way to get around. Tramlines connect major areas and transit hubs, providing a convenient and scenic way to navigate the city's congested streets.

Terminals

The following are Florence's main tram terminals:

- **Santa Maria Novella Station (SMN):** Located in the heart of the city, this terminal serves as a major hub for transportation, providing connections between regional trains, buses, taxis, and tram lines.

- **Alamanni-Stazione:** Another significant station close to Santa Maria Novella Station that offers easy access to the nearby attractions and historic core.

- **Unità:** Situated in Florence's eastern region, Unità serves as a major hub for travelers and commuters going to the airport and other suburban areas.

- **Villa Costanza**: This terminal, which is situated in Scandicci, provides access to suburban residential areas and is a major hub for tram and regional bus services.

In Florence, the cost of using the tram is typically covered by the city's public transportation system. A single tram ticket costs approximately €1.50 as of the most recent modifications, and it is valid for 90 minutes. As an alternative, visitors may buy one-day or multiple-day passes that allow them to take unlimited tram and bus excursions inside approved zones. These permits are appropriate for both transient visitors and long-term locals.

Along with practical transit, a tram ride in Florence offers an insight into the everyday activities of the city as it passes through charming neighborhoods, open-air markets, and historical landmarks. If you're traveling to a major location or just exploring Florence's rich cultural tapestry, the tram is a trustworthy and affordable way to experience everything.

Rent a scooter or moped in Florence and Tuscany.

A fun way to see Florence's streets and the gorgeous Tuscan countryside is to rent a scooter or moped. Many terminals in Florence provide scooter rentals; these include those close to major tourist attractions and transportation hubs. Rental companies are frequently located in designated locations of the city center, around train terminals, and in large piazzas like Piazza della Signoria.

The daily rental costs typically range from €30 to €50, contingent upon the scooter's model and duration of use.

Optional accessories and insurance may incur additional costs. To ensure dependable service and reasonable terms, it is advised that you compare prices and read reviews of rental companies.

Scooting through Florence and Tuscany offers independence and the chance to see hidden gems off the beaten path. Whether you're cruising through the winding streets of Florence or the undulating hills of Tuscany, renting a scooter is a fantastic way to take in the beauty and charm of the area.

Handling the Tuscany Region and Florence

Traveling through Florence and the Tuscan region is like traveling through art, history, and breathtaking scenery—every step you take reveals a new story to discover. Due to its small size, Florence is easy to explore on foot. Explore little cobblestone streets encircled by structures dating back hundreds of years, where Renaissance design blends with modern living. You can easily explore the rich history of the famous structures, including the Ponte Vecchio, which is lined with jewelry stores across the Arno River, and the Florence Cathedral, which has a stunning dome created by Brunelleschi, on foot.

There are other modes of transportation to choose from for extended excursions and exploring the broader Tuscan region. Trains provide a convenient and scenic means of transportation between Florence and important towns such as Pisa, Siena, and Lucca. Alternatively, you can explore the countryside by renting a car, where you will find old hilltop villages with their timeless charm and rolling hills covered with vineyards.

Accepting the slower pace of life that sets Tuscany apart is another necessary skill for navigating the region. Every mile spent in places like the Val d'Orcia, a UNESCO World Heritage site renowned for its breathtaking beauty, and San Gimignano, known for its medieval towers, is like traveling through a real postcard.

Whether you go by car, train, bicycle, or foot, Florence and the Tuscan region provide an adventure full of diverse activities, stunning scenery, and a wealth of cultural diversity.
Section Three. Florence's Top Attractions
Florence's Icons: The Baptistery and Duomo

Both the Baptistery and the Duomo, the Santa Maria del Fiore Cathedral, are well-known symbols of Florence, both with a magnificent history and architectural design.

Duomo (Santa Maria del Fiore Cathedral)

The Duomo, a Gothic architectural marvel rising above the metropolis, is renowned for its exquisite marble façade and Filippo Brunelleschi's distinctive red-tiled dome. Those who visit the Duomo may:

- Climb the Dome: For breathtaking views of Florence and the surrounding hills, ascend the 463 steps to the top of the dome.

- Take in the Interior: Marvel at the sculptures, stained glass windows, and paintings inside the cathedral, which include pieces by Giotto, Donatello, and Andrea del Castagno.

- Explore the Crypt: Explore the archaeological remnants of ancient Florence by going beneath the church.

The Saint John Baptistery

Nestled near to the Duomo, the Baptistery of St. John is one of Florence's oldest buildings, having been built in the eleventh century. Highlights consist of:

- **Gilded Bronze Doors**: Admire the Old Testament scenes depicted on Lorenzo Ghiberti's renowned Gates of Paradise.

- **Mosaic Ceilings**: Take in the exquisite mosaics depicting scenes from Christ's life and the Last Judgment on the Baptistery's domed ceiling.

- **Historic Significance**: Discover the history of the baptisms that occurred here for well-known Florentines, such as members of the Medici family.

Seeing the Duomo and Baptistery offers a glimpse into Florence's rich cultural past and a chance to take in the artistic and architectural magnificence of the Renaissance. These monuments serve as enduring reminders of Florence's significance as the cradle of Italian and international art and culture.

Gallery Uffizi and Accademia

Two well-known museums in Florence, the Accademia, and the Uffizi Gallery, both offer a unique perspective on the realm of art and culture that has shaped the city's past.

The Uffizi Gallery

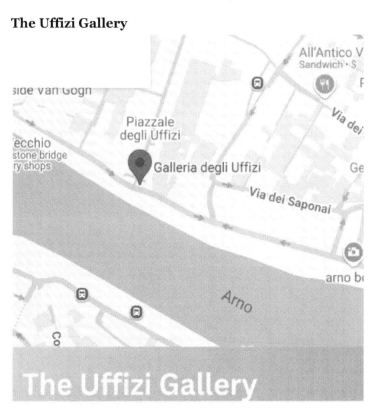

Scan the QR code

1. Open Camera: Launch your smartphone's camera app.
2. Position QR Code: Place the QR code within the camera's viewfinder.
3. Hold Steady: Keep the device steady for the camera to focus.
4. Wait for Scan: Wait for the code to be recognized.
5. Tap Notification: Follow the prompt to access the content.

Renaissance artwork abounds at the Uffizi Gallery, which is near the Piazza della Signoria. Its centuries-old collection features pieces by well-known artists like Michelangelo, Raphael, Leonardo da Vinci, and Botticelli. Visitors can view two magnificent specimens of Renaissance paintings by Botticelli, "The Birth of Venus" and "Primavera," which depict legendary themes with unparalleled beauty and accuracy. A whole narrative of Florence's creative evolution may be found in the sculptures, antiques, and paintings that line the gallery's wide hallways and intimate chambers.

The Accademia Gallery was founded in the eighteenth century and is most famous for being the home of Michelangelo's masterpiece, "David." The enormous statue of David, which was carved from a single marble block, is a representation of human beauty and achievement. In addition to "David," the Accademia is home to an incredible collection of Renaissance art, which includes works by Domenico Ghirlandaio and Sandro Botticelli. Through examining the evolution of Florentine art, visitors can gain insight into the artistic abilities and cultural significance of the Renaissance period. These exhibitions have been carefully chosen.

By visiting these museums, one can gain access to some of the most well-known pieces of art in the world as well as a deeper comprehension of Florence's cultural heritage. The Uffizi Gallery and Accademia invite visitors to engage deeply and profoundly with history and creativity through an immersive journey through Florence's artistic essence, showcasing everything from the exquisite intricacies of Michelangelo's sculptures to the ethereal beauty of Botticelli's paintings.

The Palazzo Vecchio and Ponte Vecchio

The historic Ponte Vecchio

An everlasting symbol of Florence's architectural brilliance and historical significance is the Ponte Vecchio. This historic bridge, which crosses the serene Arno River, enthralls visitors with its unusual design and extensive cultural heritage. Rebuilt in the 14th century, the bridge dates back to Roman times and is renowned for the distinctive stores that flank its edges. Set against the backdrop of the river below, these shops, formerly occupied by jewelers, offer a vivid mosaic of colors and craftsmanship. Strolling across the Ponte Vecchio offers breathtaking views of Florence's skyline along with a glimpse into the city's past as a center of commerce and culture.

The historic Palazzo Vecchio

Nestled in the center of Florence's historic area, Palazzo Vecchio is a major reminder of the city's rich political and cultural past. The Palazzo Vecchio has long served as the center of Florentine power. It was first constructed as a fortress palace in the late 13th century. Its splendid façade, adorned with elaborate sculptures and crenellations, highlights the bustling Piazza della Signoria. The lavish chambers of Palazzo Vecchio, which are decorated with murals by well-known painters including Giorgio Vasari and Cosimo Roselli, are open for tours. The palace's largest hall, Salone dei Cinquecento, features enormous artworks and stunning ceilings that symbolize Florence's support of the arts during the Renaissance.

Features and Expectations for Guests:

- **Ponte Vecchio**: Walk across the bridge to take in the sparkling Arno River and the historic buildings.

Admire the shops for exquisite jewelry and awe-inspiring skyline views of Florence.

- **Palazzo Vecchio**: Take a guided tour to learn about the history of the palace and explore the inside to view Renaissance artworks, such as Michelangelo's famous sculpture "Genius of Victory." Climb the tower for panoramic views of Florence.

Scan the QR code

1. Open Camera: Launch your smartphone's camera app.
2. Position QR Code: Place the QR code within the camera's viewfinder.
3. Hold Steady: Keep the device steady for the camera to focus.
4. Wait for Scan: Wait for the code to be recognized.
5. Tap Notification: Follow the prompt to access the content.

The Ponte Vecchio and the Palazzo Vecchio, which invite visitors to immerse themselves in the city's rich cultural past, are symbols of Florence's blend of artistic innovation and architectural magnificence.

Pitti Palace and the Boboli Gardens

Boboli Garden:

Boboli Garden

Scan the QR code

1. Open Camera: Launch your smartphone's camera app.
2. Position QR Code: Place the QR code within the camera's viewfinder.
3. Hold Steady: Keep the device steady for the camera to focus.
4. Wait for Scan: Wait for the code to be recognized.
5. Tap Notification: Follow the prompt to access the content.

The Boboli Gardens are a prime example of Florence's masterful fusion of artistry and environment. These 111 acres of expansive gardens, which are situated behind Pitti Palace, were created in the sixteenth century. Designed to resemble a large Medici garden, the Boboli Gardens have well-manicured grass, an abundance of lush foliage, and a wide range of flora, including old trees, exquisite flowers, and intricate fountains. Strolling along walkways shaded by sculptures and architectural marvels, visitors may take in new views of Florence's skyline and the undulating hills beyond at every bend. The gardens' tiered layout provides expansive views of the city, turning it into a peaceful haven amidst the busy metropolis.

Pitti Palace:

The Pitti Palace, which stands at the gateway to the Boboli Gardens, is a symbol of Florence's rich cultural heritage and opulence. The magnificent Medici dynasty first resided in the palace, which was first built in the fifteenth century for the Pitti family. Its imposing façade, with its perfect proportions and Renaissance style, exudes a regal presence in Piazza Pitti. The Pitti Palace offers visitors the chance to peruse its vast galleries and exquisite apartments, each of which displays a singular collection of artwork spanning several centuries. Highlights include works of art by Rubens, Titian, and Raphael as well as exquisite ornamental arts and antique furniture that shed light on the luxurious way of life of Florence's nobility.

Features and Expectations for Guests:

- **Boboli Gardens**: Stroll over statue-lined, centuries-old walks shaded by old trees. Explore hidden caves, bubbling springs, and expansive overlooks offering breathtaking panoramas of Florence and the surrounding countryside.

- **Pitti Palace**: Explore the opulent interiors of the palace, which include the Palatine Gallery and the Royal Apartments, which are home to priceless works of European and Italian art. For more information on the evolution of fashion in Florence and beyond, see the Museum of Costume & Fashion.

Visitors can learn about Florence's aristocratic heritage and its rich cultural legacy by visiting the Pitti Palace and Boboli Gardens. Discovering Florence and appreciating its timeless beauty are encouraged by its popular attractions, which range from serene garden strolls to immersive art experiences.

Chapter 4. Seeing the Tuscan region

History and Highlights of Siena.

History and Highlights of Siena.

Nestled amidst the undulating hills of Tuscany, Siena beckons tourists with its spectacular beauty and rich historical legacy. This historic city, founded by the Etruscans and developed into a thriving hub during the Middle Ages, has managed to hold onto its distinctive Gothic architecture and cultural customs. Throughout its history, Siena and Florence have engaged in bitter rivalry as they battled for control of the region, shaping its political and cultural landscape.

Established under the Roman Empire, Siena flourished as a significant intersection and economic center. Throughout the Middle Ages, its fortunes improved as it developed into a powerful city-state renowned for its cultural patronage and banking acumen. The battle of Montaperti in 1260, which solidified Siena's independence and marked a turning point in its history, was the result of the fight with Florence.

The 13th and 14th centuries, known as Siena's golden age, saw the construction of the city's most notable buildings, such as the imposing Duomo di Siena and the Palazzo Pubblico. With their intricate sculptures, vivid paintings, and exquisite details that showcase the craftsmanship of the era, these architectural marvels stand for the wealth and ambition of the city.

Standouts:

- **Piazza del Campo**: Located in the heart of Siena, this medieval square is one of the best in all of

33

Europe. Its distinctive shell shape, encircled by historic structures and crowned by the Palazzo Pubblico, is home to the thrilling twice-yearly Palio di Siena horse race, a 17th-century custom.

- **Siena Cathedral (Duomo di Siena):** The magnificent exterior of this Gothic masterpiece is adorned with intricate marble statues and carvings. Visitors are enthralled by the exquisite interiors, especially the Piccolomini Library with its collection of paintings by Pinturicchio and its exquisite mosaic floor that vividly illustrates biblical stories.

- **Palazzo Pubblico**: This 14th-century building has been Siena's government headquarters, a testament to the city's support for the arts and political might. The stunning murals by Ambrogio Lorenzetti in the Sala della Pace (Room of Peace), which depict allegories of both excellent and bad governance, are among the highlights.

- **Siena's Contrade**: The city is divided into seventeen districts, or Contrade, each with its own unique culture. For those who want to witness the intense sense of community that permeates Siena, the Palio is a must-see event. It is an exhilarating display of local pride and traditional customs, as these Contrade battle fiercely.

Every square and street in Siena tells a story of the city's cultural heritage and historical grandeur, visiting there feels like a voyage through time. Immersion in Siena's rich past and vibrant present is encouraged by the city's breathtaking architecture and vibrant traditions.

Leaning Tower of Pisa and Beyond.

The charming city of Pisa, which is in the center of Tuscany, is well-known across the world for both its extensive historical past and its iconic Leaning Tower. Pisa, which is situated on the Arno River's banks, enthralls visitors with its magnificent architecture, vibrant culture, and stellar academic reputation.

The Pisa Leaning Tower:

The Leaning Tower of Pisa is proof of both human ingenuity and bad building design. Constructed over two centuries, starting in the 12th century, this bell tower's inadvertent tilt has elevated it to a global symbol of resilience and technological marvels. The tower's beautiful white marble facade, with its arches and columns, exudes timeless elegance despite its lean. Climbers can take the spiral staircase to the top of the tower, where they can take in expansive views of Pisa and the surrounding area, offering a singular viewpoint of this historic city.

Beyond the Tower of Leaning:

Beyond its well-known monument, Pisa entices tourists to discover the city's rich cultural and historical tapestry. A UNESCO World Heritage site, the Leaning Tower is situated amidst the Campo dei Miracoli (Field of Miracles), which is also home to the imposing Pisa Cathedral and the St. John's Baptistery. These works of art demonstrate the inventiveness of the architects as well as the medieval magnificence of Pisa.

Investigate Pisa:

Past the Campo dei Miracoli, Pisa beckons with its charming lanes lined with historic homes, lively cafés, and bustling marketplaces. The city's university, one of the oldest in Europe and founded in 1343, gives the surroundings a youthful, intellectually stimulating energy. Wander the Arno River, cross historic bridges, and find undiscovered treasures tucked away in Pisa's winding alleyways.

Delights of culture:

Pisa boasts a bustling cultural scene, with theaters, galleries, and museums honoring the city's scientific and artistic heritage. The Museo dell'Opera del Duomo houses an antiques and medieval sculpture collection, while the Palazzo Blu hosts contemporary art exhibitions and cultural activities.

Treasures from the kitchen:

Without enjoying Pisa's culinary delights, a visit is not complete. Classic Tuscan dishes like ribollita (vegetable soup), cecina (chickpea flatbread), and Pisa's special spin on pasta and seafood delights are served at neighborhood trattorias. The features of the region pair well with a drink of Chianti, or other famous Tuscan wine.

With the Leaning Tower serving as a lighthouse, Pisa invites visitors to discover its rich past, rejoice in its diversity of cultures, and experience the timeless beauty of Tuscany. Beyond the well-known landmark is a city full of undiscovered treasures and life-changing experiences.

Lucca: Historic Walls and Uptown Elegance

Lucca, which is ideally situated in the center of Tuscany, transports visitors on an enthralling journey through time and culture by skillfully fusing its rich historical legacy with modern pleasures. Lucca exhibits its medieval past and strategic importance, enclosed by walls that date back to the Renaissance. Originally built as a barrier against invaders, these enormous walls are now a spectacular promenade that offers sweeping views of the city and its surroundings.

Within the boundaries of these historic defenses is a bustling metropolis full of natural beauty. Since cars are not allowed inside the city walls, the best ways to explore Lucca's historic center are on foot or by bicycle. The ancient core is lined with charming piazzas and narrow cobblestone streets. Romanesque cathedrals, Gothic palaces, and imposing towers that showcase the city's rich architectural heritage are all on display. The city has long been a center of trade and culture.

Lucca in the modern era draws visitors with its vibrant cultural scene and mouthwatering cuisine. The renowned Lucca Summer Festival, which attracts music lovers from all over the world, is one of the city's many annual festivals and events. There are numerous art galleries, stores, and cafés lining the streets where you may discover traditional handicrafts and savor regional specialties like Buccellato (sweet bread).

Beyond its city limits, Lucca is a wonderful destination with stunning countryside dotted with olive orchards and vineyards just a short drive away. Tourists can stroll around the Giardini Pfanner, bike around the city's medieval defenses, or climb the Torre Guinigi for sweeping views of the city and hills beyond.

Lucca charms with its blend of the past and present, whether one is steeped in its rich history, enjoying its culinary delights, or taking in its vibrant cultural scene. Lucca is a city that blends ancient elegance with modern vibrancy. It encourages visitors to stroll its streets, find hidden gems, and feel the essence of Tuscany.

San Gimignano, known as the Tower Town

Known as the "Town of Towers," San Gimignano is a quaint village tucked away among the undulating hills of Tuscany. This hilltop medieval town is well-known for its dramatic skyline, which is made up of fourteen historic towers that tower majestically over the surrounding area. The towers of San Gimignano were originally built in the 12th and 13th centuries as symbols of power and grandeur by wealthy families. The city was once a bustling center of trade and business along the Via Francigena.

Today, these remarkably intact towers provide visitors a glimpse into the town's magnificent architecture and act as a reminder of San Gimignano's wealthy past. With every bend in the narrow cobblestone alleyways dotted with historic buildings, you are treated to a new perspective of these exquisite buildings set against the backdrop of Tuscany.

San Gimignano enthralls tourists with its rich history and cultural heritage in addition to its striking towers. A tangle of historic streets and charming squares, the old town has been recognized as a UNESCO World Heritage site since 1990. See the remnants of a 13th-century well at Piazza della Cisterna, or stop by the Collegiate Church of Santa Maria Assunta, which boasts beautiful artwork and Romanesque architecture.

In addition, San Gimignano is well-known for its delectable cuisine, which features the region's signature gelato and wine, Vernaccia di San Gimignano. Cafes and trattorias entice you with regional specialties, allowing you to sample Tuscan cuisine while taking in the town's enduring ambiance.

San Gimignano offers an amazing journey through time and tradition in the center of Tuscany, whether you come to take in the breathtaking skyline, immerse yourself in history, or just enjoy the laid-back pace of life in this historic gem.

Chianti Area: Wine and Rural Landscape

Tuscany's Chianti region emerges like a pastoral masterpiece, with undulating hills adorned with olive and vineyard trees, resembling a scene from a Renaissance painting. Between Florence and Siena, this well-known wine-growing region is renowned for producing some of Italy's best wines in addition to its pastoral charm and delectable cuisine.

Scenery Beauty

It feels like you are driving over a live painting when you are in the Chianti region. Vineyards blanket the hills; their hues shift with the seasons, producing a breathtaking palette of gold and green. Historic roads that wind past hilltop communities are lined with cypress trees, and around every bend, there's a new, expansive view of centuries-old farmhouses and hillsides covered in vines.

Wineries and vineyards:

Chianti is known for its excellent wines, especially the Chianti Classico DOCG. When you visit the region, you will find family-owned vineyards tucked away in picturesque settings, where generations of winemakers have passed down their skills. While visiting these estates, you may taste award-winning wines and discover the meticulous farming and aging techniques that give each bottle its distinct flavor.

Delights in cuisine:

Chianti is known for its wines, but it's also known for its fresh, regional cuisine. A variety of classic Tuscan dishes, including warmly served pecorino cheese, wild boar ragu, and ribollita (a bean soup), are offered in rustic trattorias and osterias. Another well-known local product that gives every meal a rich flavor and golden hue is olive oil.

Villages with a history:

Discovering the Chianti region means coming across historic communities that appear to be frozen in time. Greve in Chianti serves as the entry point to the region with its stunning Piazza Matteotti and historic churches. With its impressive fortress walls and Etruscan ancestry, Castellina offers a glimpse into the past. The peaceful ambiance of Radda, a hilltop village encircled by vineyards, invites leisurely exploration.

Peace and hospitality:

Beyond its abundance of natural and cultural resources, the Chianti region is a haven of friendliness and tranquility. Visitors can experience the slower pace of life in the area by booking accommodations in the countryside at boutique hotels or agriturismos (farm stays). Here, time appears to slow down, allowing for peaceful times spent surrounded by the splendor of the natural world and the welcoming warmth of Tuscany.

Tuscany's Chianti region is an experience that awakens the senses and uplifts the soul, not just a place to visit. Every minute spent in Chianti is a celebration of life's little joys and the timeless beauty of Italy's countryside, whether you're sipping wine while taking in the views of hills covered in vines or having a typical lunch outside under the sun.

Chapter 5. Historical Sites

Ancient Roman Amphitheater at Fiesole: Immaculate Ruins

The Roman Amphitheatre of Fiesole, tucked away in the peaceful hillsides overlooking Florence, is a reminder of the colorful past of the ancient city. This first-century BC archaeological wonder offers tourists a glimpse into the opulence and spectacle of Roman entertainment.

The semi-circular shape of the amphitheater sets it apart from other Roman arenas of the era. It was originally the site of public assemblies, theater performances, and gladiatorial contests for the ancient Fiesole citizens. It was carved into the hillside's natural slope. The building's stone tiers and remnants of seating arrangements capture the spirit of the event's golden age when spectators cheered and yelled against a backdrop of Tuscan landscapes.

Wandering around the immaculate remnants, visitors may relive the noise of the crowd and the slashing of swords that once filled the arena. The significance of the location as a cultural hub in ancient Etruria is emphasized by informative plaques that describe the site's history and architecture. In addition, the nearby archeological site offers breathtaking vistas of the Tuscan countryside and artifacts from Roman baths and temples.

The Fiesole Roman Amphitheatre invites guests to travel back in time by offering a glimpse into the customs and cultural artifacts of a bygone era. It is a somber reminder of the lengthy history of Fiesole and its place in the intricate web of Italian archeological resources.

A historic marvel in Tuscany is the Roman Theatre in Lucca.

Lucca's Roman Theatre is a prime example of the city's rich architectural and historical legacy. In the gorgeous surrounds of contemporary Lucca, this well-preserved antique theater from the first century BC offers visitors a glimpse into ancient Roman artistic life.

Situated in Lucca's historic center, the Roman Theatre is a striking structure in terms of both its size and historical significance. Up to 10,000 spectators could once fit within the semi-circular theater, which was built into a natural land slope and hosted theatrical productions, gladiatorial fights, and other public events. The seating area (cave), stage (pulpit), and backstage (scaenae frons) are all well-preserved portions of the archeological site that demonstrate the masterful architectural design of the Roman builders.

When visiting the Roman Theatre of Lucca, visitors can travel back in time by exploring the ancient ruins and seeing the vibrant cultural scenes that formerly took place there. The location offers educational displays and guided tours that cover the history of theater and its significance in Roman society. The old stones below are beautifully framed by expansive views of the surrounding hills and the roofs of Lucca, which may be seen from the upper levels of the cave.

Discovering Lucca's Roman Theatre offers a singular fusion of cultural enrichment and archaeological interest, enabling guests to engage with the city's past while appreciating its contemporary attractiveness.

Rome's Caracalla Baths: Historic Magnificence.

An enormous testament to the splendor and engineering of ancient Rome is the Baths of Caracalla. Constructed in the third century AD under the reign of Emperor Caracalla, these enormous public baths served as a hub for social and cultural activities in ancient Rome. They are now among the most amazing archaeological sites in the city, giving visitors a glimpse into the opulent way of life led by the Romans.

Qualities:

The vast scale and magnificent architecture of the Baths of Caracalla are well-known. Covering an area of around 25 acres, the complex consists of:

- **Central Bathing Complex:** The central area of the baths, including spacious passageways and tall vaulted ceilings held up by ornate stonework. There was a large cold-water pool in the frigidarium, the main hall, where bathers could relax and chat.

- **Gym and workout areas**: The main swimming area is encircled by expansive grounds that were formerly home to outdoor gardens, workout areas, and even libraries where visitors could engage in both intellectual and physical activities.

- **Mosaic flooring and Ornate Elements:** The complex was formerly lavishly ornamented, as evidenced by the remnants of intricate mosaic flooring, marble columns, and ornate sculptures found throughout the baths.

What Guests Can Investigate

- **Central Halls**: Take a stroll through the frigidarium and other big halls, imagining the bustling atmosphere of the ancient Romans as they mixed and enjoyed the curative waters in these enormous spaces.

- **Gardens and Exercise** Areas: Take a tour of the expansive gardens, which are now adorned with the remnants of ancient statues and offer peaceful havens amidst the ruins.

- **Ancient Technology**: Learn about the incredible Roman engineering that made it possible for the water to be heated and distributed around the baths.

A fascinating look into ancient Roman life, a visit to the Baths of Caracalla offers visitors an opportunity to witness the artistic and architectural achievements of a time when the pursuit of physical well-being and societal cohesion was valued highly.

Roman Forum in Rome: An Exploration of Ancient Times.

Rome's Roman Forum offers visitors a glimpse into the inner workings of one of the greatest civilizations in history and is a wonderful reminder of the splendor of ancient Rome. This massive archaeological complex served as the political, religious, and commercial center of the Roman Empire for centuries, a hive of activity and life at its height.

Qualities:

The Roman Forum is an amazing collection of enormous monuments and ruins that formerly represented daily life in ancient Rome. Highlights consist of:

- **The Temple of Saturn**: Dedicated to the god of agriculture and wealth, the ruins of this temple are made up of eight tall columns that allude to its former splendor.

- **The Arch of Septimius Severus**: An ornate relief depicting military prowess adorns this triumphal arch, which honors Emperor Septimius Severus' accomplishments.

- The Senate House, or Curia Julia: It was were Roman senators debated and enacted laws, offering a window into the political intrigues of classical Rome.

- **The Temple of Vesta**: An old circular temple dedicated to the goddess of the hearth, who stands for the enduring power of the Roman Empire.

- **The Rostra**: A stage where speakers addressed the Roman populace, featuring well-known orations by Julius Caesar and Cicero.

What Guests Can Investigate

The Roman Forum offers visitors the opportunity to fully immerse themselves in the remnants of Roman governance and daily life.

- Take a stroll along the Sacred Way, also known as the Via Sacra, which served as the main thoroughfare for triumphant processions and religious ceremonies in ancient Rome.

- Take a tour of Palatine Hill, which is adjacent to the Forum and offers sweeping views of the Circus Maximus, imperial structures, and gardens.

- **Go to the Archaeological Museum**: Located on the premises, it features artifacts unearthed from the Forum and neighboring sites, providing background information on the history of the area.

- **Take a Nighttime Tour of the Roman Forum**: A few trips include visits in the evening, which offer a distinctive perspective of the ruins against the backdrop of the city lights.

The Roman Forum is more than just ruins; it is a dynamic reminder of the power, resourcefulness, and cultural diversity of classical Rome. Travelers can step back in time and engage with the legacy of one of the greatest civilizations in history by exploring its ruins.

masterworks from the Renaissance

Renaissance art is replete with masterpieces that perfectly capture the innovation and cultural brilliance of the time.

These sculptures evoke a period of creative regeneration and humanistic research with their immaculate accuracy, vivid hues, and profound meaning.

"The Last Supper" by Leonardo Da Vinci:

This iconic fresco painting at Santa Maria delle Grazie church in Milan depicts the poignant conversation Jesus had with his disciples just before his crucifixion. Leonardo's command of human emotion and perspective is evident, drawing viewers into the dramatic atmosphere of the action.

Leonardo da Vinci's "David"

The Accademia Gallery in Florence's marble sculpture "David" embodies the Renaissance ideals of grace, strength, and ideal proportions. With meticulous carving, Michelangelo transforms a block of solid stone into a dynamic sculpture that represents David's courage and determination before his battle with Goliath.

Raphael's "The School of Athens":

Housed in the Apostolic Palace in the Vatican, this artwork is a prime example of Raphael's skill in fusing Renaissance ideals with ancient concepts. The image depicts a gathering of classical Greek philosophers against a grand architectural background, each one exuding focus and brilliance.

"Venus of Urbino" by Titian:

Venus is shown in this provocative image from Florence's Uffizi Gallery, sultry as she lounges on a bed, celebrating femininity and sensuality. Titian's use of texture and color creates an opulent atmosphere that inspires viewers to reflect on matters of desire and love.

The "Baptism of Christ" by Verrocchio:

This collaborative piece by Verrocchio and Leonardo da Vinci, housed in Florence's Uffizi Gallery, demonstrates Verrocchio's skill with narrative organization and dramatic movement. The image shows the pivotal moment of John the Baptist's baptism of Christ, with people glowing softly and displaying emotive gestures.

These Renaissance classics exhibit technical mastery, artistic innovation, and intellectual, cultural, and spiritual aims that were central to the Renaissance movement. They still arouse awe and reverence in onlookers, encouraging them to consider the enduring beauty and profound lessons of this pivotal historical era.

Chapter 6. Culture and Art

Galleries and Museums

Florence's Bargello National Museum

Renaissance ornamental arts and sculpture are housed in a medieval fortress in Florence's Bargello National Museum. The Bargello, which was first a fortification and subsequently a jail, is now home to an amazing collection of paintings dating from the fourteenth to the seventeenth centuries.

Qualities:

- **Sculpture Collection**: The museum features an exquisite collection of sculptures by well-known artists, including Michelangelo's "Bacchus" and Donatello's "David." Other notable artists include Cellini and Michelangelo.

- **Decorative Arts**: Visitors can view superb examples of the decorative arts, including jewelry, textiles, and pottery, which showcase the Renaissance period's artistry and innovation.

- **Courtyard**: The museum's statue-adorned courtyard, which is shaded by a stunning tower, offers a tranquil place to relax and take in Bargello's stunning architectural design.

What Guests Can Investigate

- **Donatello's David**: Take a look at Donatello's ground-breaking sculpture of David, whose dynamic attitude and lifelike portrayal revolutionized Renaissance art.

- **Michelangelo's early sculpture of Bacchus:** This work demonstrates the artist's knowledge of anatomy and emotion and hints at the talent that would eventually yield David and Pietà.

- **Temporary exhibits**: The Bargello frequently hosts one-time displays that shed light on certain facets of Renaissance culture and art.

A voyage through the artistic glories of Renaissance Florence can be had by visiting the Bargello National Museum, where each masterpiece evokes reflection on the inventiveness and skill of this transformative historical period.

The Institute and Museum of the History of Science in Florence is called Museo Galileo.

Situated in the heart of Florence, the Museo Galileo is an enchanting establishment that celebrates the achievements of renowned scientist and astronomer Galileo Galilei as well as the history of science. This museum transports guests through decades of scientific advancement while preserving its historic surroundings to spark the interest of the mind.

Qualities:

- **Galileo's tools**: The museum is home to an amazing array of scientific tools, including telescopes, astrolabes, and early experimental instruments that Galileo personally used.

- **Globes & Maps**: Explore intricate celestial globes and terrestrial maps from many historical periods that illustrate the development of cartography and our understanding of the cosmos.

- **Scientific Artifacts**: Examine a wide range of scientific artifacts, such as early medical instruments and mechanical creations that show off advancements in mathematics, physics, and astronomy.

- **Interactive exhibitions**: Visitors can explore and learn through hands-on activities in interactive exhibitions that bring scientific concepts to life.

What Guests Can Investigate

- **Galileo's Telescopes**: View the authentic and replica telescopes that Galileo used to make important astronomical observations, such as his examination of Jupiter's moons.

- **Historical Context**: Discover the intellectual and cultural milieu of Renaissance Florence, a time when luminaries like Galileo revolutionized our understanding of the natural world.

- **Temporary Exhibitions**: Take in ever-changing displays that delve into certain scientific subjects or bring attention to lesser-known facets of Galileo's life and contributions.

- **Educational Programs**: Gain a deeper comprehension of the intersection of science, history, and culture by attending lectures, seminars, and guided tours available to guests of all ages.

For those interested in the wonders of nature and the legacy of Galileo Galilei, the Museo Galileo offers a singular opportunity to explore the development of scientific inquiry and innovation.

Inside the historic San Salvi monastery complex, Florence's Museum of San Salvi offers a tranquil escape from the bustling city center. This undiscovered gem boasts a large collection of historical artifacts and religious artwork, including sculptures and artifacts from archeological digs. The museum's refectory and serene cloister, which have murals depicting events from Saint Benedict's life, are its attractions. In addition, the museum hosts temporary exhibitions that delve into various facets of Florentine history and culture, providing a peaceful haven away from the bustle of the city's rich creative past.

Saint Maria of Fiore Opera Museum in Florence

Adjacent to Florence's famous Duomo, the Museum of Opera del Duomo (Museo dell'Opera del Duomo)

It offers tourists a comprehensive look at the artwork and background of one of Italy's most well-known cathedrals. The exquisite sculptures, original stained glass windows, and architectural models highlight the passion and artistry that have shaped the Duomo's evolution over time.

Qualities:

- **genuine Artworks**: The museum is home to genuine artworks, like sculptures by well-known artists like Michelangelo and Donatello, that were once used to adorn the Duomo.

- **Architectural Models**: Visitors can examine intricate models that illustrate the Duomo's several design and construction phases as well as its recognizable dome.

- **Ghiberti's Doors**: Famous bronze doors by Ghiberti, most notably the Gates of Paradise, which magnificently depict Old Testament subjects in relief, are on display.

- **Stained Glass**: The museum preserves and presents its original stained glass windows, which feature deft artistry and vivid hues that illuminate the interior cathedral.

- **Historical artifacts**: An assortment of artifacts from the past, such as instruments and documents, illuminates the challenges and achievements faced in building one of the biggest cathedrals in history.

What Guests Can Investigate

- **Sculpture Gallery**: See pieces like Michelangelo's incomplete Pieta and Donatello's eerie Penitent Magdalene that formerly adorned the Duomo's façade.

- **Educational exhibitions**: Take part in interactive displays that delve into the cultural significance of Florence's cathedral complex as well as the technical marvels of Brunelleschi's dome.

- **Views from the Terrace:** Climb the museum's terrace for expansive views of Florence's skyline, which includes Giotto's Bell Tower and Brunelleschi's imposing dome.

Gain a deeper grasp of Florence's cultural history and artistic achievements by exploring the creative legacy and architectural brilliance that support the city's most famous cathedral, the Museum of Opera del Duomo.

Celebrations & Occasions

The Palio in Siena.

Twice a year, in the heart of Siena, Tuscany, is the centuries-old Palio di Siena horse race. The combination of history, spectacle, and fierce competition makes this event, which takes place on July 2nd (Palio di Provenzano) and August 16th (Palio dell'Assunta), enthralling locals and visitors alike.

The Palio is a celebration of Siena's history and community spirit, not just a horse race. Ten of the seventeen Contrade (districts) of Siena compete in the race; each is represented by a jockey who circles the Piazza del Campo, the main square in the city, on horseback. The race is short—about ninety seconds—but days of colorful extravaganza—parades, feasts, and medieval traditions—precede it.

Twice a year, the Palio di Siena takes place:

- **July 2nd**: The Madonna of Provenzano is honored at the Palio di Provenzano.

- **August 16**: Mary's Assumption is celebrated at the Palio dell'Assunta.

Thousands of people turn out these days to see the excitement and passion of one of Italy's most well-known and beloved cultural events.

San Ranieri Luminara (Pisa).

Every year, Pisa celebrates the Luminara di San Ranieri, a beautiful event that pays homage to San Ranieri, the city's patron saint. This intriguing event transforms Pisa's historic buildings and the banks of the Arno River into a breathtaking light show on the evening of June 16th.

Qualities:

- **Candlelit Displays**: The bridges, castles, cathedrals, and towers along the Arno River are adorned with thousands of candles, which create a beautiful reflection on the water below.

- **Historic Buildings**: The stunning display adds to the architectural magnificence of Pisa's notable landmarks, especially the well-known Leaning Tower, by illuminating them with a warm glow.

- **Procession and Fireworks**: The festivities culminate in a stunning fireworks display that lights up Pisa's night sky, after a solemn procession through the city's streets.

Every year on June 16th in the evening, residents and visitors alike converge on Pisa's heart for the Luminara di San Ranieri, a captivating celebration of light, tradition, and community spirit.

Historic Florence Calcio

Every year, Florence, Italy hosts Calcio Storico, also referred to as "historical football," an unusual and historic sporting event. Originating in the sixteenth century, this ancient sport combines elements of rugby, football, and wrestling to create a spectacle that is both athletic and rich in culture.

June is typically the month for Calcio Storico celebrations, especially in the days leading up to and including June 24th, the feast day of San Giovanni, also known as Saint John the Baptist, who is Florence's patron saint.

Four teams—Santa Croce (blue), Santa Maria Novella (red), Santo Spirito (white), and San Giovanni (green)—represent different neighborhoods in Florence throughout the game. Each squad, consisting of 27 men, plays on a field covered in sand in Piazza Santa Croce. Tossing the ball into the opponent's goal, which is placed on each end of the field, is how points are scored.

Calcio Storico is a cultural festival that attracts both locals and tourists, and it's more than just a sporting event. There is a dramatic and raucous atmosphere as supporters vociferously cheer for their home clubs. Dressed in Renaissance attire, the competitors demonstrate their physical prowess as well as their strategic play.

Calcio Storico is a highly competitive sport in Florence with a rich historical background. It stands for the city's pride in the community and competitive sports, which are rooted in its medieval and Renaissance heritage. An essential part of Florence's cultural identity, the event upholds centuries-old traditions.

With its captivating spectacle that blends history, sport, and local culture, Calcio Storico offers an intriguing look into Florence's past and present.

Summer Festival in Lucca, Italy

An annual music festival called the Lucca Summer Event takes place in the charming Tuscan city of Lucca. Fans of music from all over the world travel to this festival to witness performances by well-known artists from a variety of genres. With Lucca's historic walls and picturesque squares as a backdrop, the festival offers a special blend of musical enjoyment and cultural immersion.

Traditionally, the Lucca Summer Festival takes place during the summer, most notably in June and July. With Lucca's stunning settings and ancient architecture serving as a backdrop, the festival experience is enhanced by the guests' ability to take advantage of mild nights and outdoor music.

Lucca comes alive with a festive atmosphere during the festival as music reverberates through its squares and streets,

creating lifelong memories for those who come to take in music in one of Tuscany's most picturesque locations.
Viareggio Carnival.

Every year, the beach town of Viareggio, Tuscany, hosts one of the most renowned and extravagant festivals in Italy: the Viareggio Carnival. This vibrant celebration, which dates back to the late 1800s, is well-known for its enormous paper-mâché sculptures, colorful parade floats, and vibrant costumes that light up the streets with energy and color.

Traditionally, the Viareggio Carnival takes place in February or March, with festivities extending over several weeks before Ash Wednesday, also known as Shrove Tuesday, or Fat Tuesday.

Qualities:

- **Parade Floats**: Stunning floats, some of which are more than 20 meters tall, depict humorous and satirical scenarios based on current affairs, politics, and popular culture.

- **Papier-Mâché sculptures**: Artists carve enormous paper-mâché sculptures known as "burlamacco," each of which represents a different subject or character and adds to the festive atmosphere of the carnival.

- **Costumed Participants**: Thousands of locals and visitors alike adorn vibrant masks and costumes to participate in the procession and heighten the joyous spirit of the carnival.

- **Entertainment & Music**: A carnival atmosphere fit for all ages is created as the streets come alive with music, dancing performances, and street vendors serving authentic Tuscan fare.

A major cultural attraction in Tuscany, the Viareggio Carnival attracts tourists from all over the world who come to witness creative brilliance, group fervor, and exuberant celebration during the week leading up to Lent.

Regional Workshops and Artists

In Tuscany, regional artisans and craft centers stand for a long history of skill and artistic innovation. These skilled artisans contribute to the distinctive cultural fabric of the area by creating handcrafted objects that embody both modernity and heritage.

Craftsman Customs:
Many crafts, including as ceramics, leatherworking, glassblowing, woodwork, and textile weaving, are areas of expertise for Tuscan artists. Every craft has its own history and set of customs, usually derived from centuries-old customs that have evolved through time.

Studios & Workshops:
It is possible to witness firsthand the meticulous work that goes into creating these beautiful objects by visiting workshops and studios. From small, family-run studios in medieval towns to larger ateliers in urban areas, every workshop offers a window into the passion and skill required to produce fine handcrafted goods.

Expertise In Motion:

In these courses, artists work with raw materials to make art. Examples of this type of work include blowing molten glass into delicate sculptures, sewing leather into wonderfully constructed bags, and sculpting clay on a potter's wheel. Craftsmen in the area are highly creative, drawing inspiration from the history, cultural legacy, and landscapes of Tuscany.

Regional fairs and markets:
Artists can advertise and sell their goods to the general public directly at the markets and fairs across Tuscany. These gatherings of artisans and enthusiasts for locally made, handcrafted goods serve to showcase craftsmanship.

Maintaining cultural legacy:
Travelers contribute to the preservation of Tuscany's handcrafted tradition by purchasing goods from local artisans. Every purchase ensures that these craftsmen continue to grow and thrive in the modern world, while still supporting traditional crafts.

Visiting Tuscany's artisanal workshops lets tourists engage with the stories and skills that go into each handcrafted masterpiece, which enhances one's awareness of the inventiveness and cultural richness of the region.

Chapter 7. Culinary pleasures

typical food from Tuscany

Bollita

The hearty, flavorful classic Tuscan soup known as rigoleta embodies the rustic cuisine of the area. This dish was first created as a way to use up leftover bread and vegetables, and both locals and visitors enjoyed its pleasant and healthful meal.

Cannellini beans, kale or cabbage, carrots, celery, onions, and tomatoes are combined to make the thick soup known as rigoleta. The ingredients are sautéed in olive oil and flavored with herbs that add flavor. The use of stale bread, which is added to the soup and cooked until it breaks down and thickens the liquid, sets ribollita apart.

Where ribollita is served affects how much it costs. In Tuscany, ribollita is a cheap and satisfying option for both locals and tourists seeking authentically prepared Tuscan food. A bowl typically costs between €5 and €10 at a small trattoria or osteria.

The robust flavors and nutritious components of rigolita encapsulate the essence of classic Tuscan cooking, offering a wonderful and reasonably priced supper that pays homage to the area's culinary heritage.

A popular dish in Tuscany, bistecca alla Fiorentina consists of a thick-cut T-bone steak from Chianina cattle that are raised nearby. Perfectly grilled over a wood fire, it boasts a charred exterior and a juicy, tender inside that is seasoned with a small amount of salt, pepper, and olive oil. For this culinary marvel to keep its original flavors and succulent texture, it is typically served rare or medium-rare.

The cost of Bistecca alla Fiorentina varies significantly depending on the restaurant and the size of the steak, but in Florence's best eateries, the budget is between €50 and €70 per kilogram.

Papa di Pomodoro.

The emphasis of the traditional Tuscan dish Pappa al Pomodoro is on comfort and simplicity. This hearty tomato and bread soup pays homage to the area's culinary customs by blending basic ingredients to create a satisfying and delicious meal.

Stale bread is soaked in a flavorful tomato broth that includes garlic, onions, olive oil, and fresh basil to make Pappa al Pomodoro. The rich, velvety soup is made thick and substantial with the bread soaking up the aromatics. Fresh basil leaves and a drizzle of extra virgin olive oil are frequently added while serving, giving each bite a burst of freshness.

Pappa al Pomodoro costs differ depending on the eatery or trattoria. Depending on the location and atmosphere of the restaurant, expect to pay between €8 and €15 per dish.

This famous Tuscan supper, which features distinctive Tuscan ingredients in every mouthful, is not only a culinary delight but also a cultural symbol of inventiveness and simplicity.

Lampredotto: a specialty from Tuscany

A traditional dish from Florence that embodies the region's culinary traditions and love of nose-to-tail cooking is lampredotto. The fourth stomach of a cow is used to make lampredotto, which is cooked gently until soft in a broth of tomatoes, onions, and aromatic herbs. It offers a flavorful and rich gastronomic experience when it is thinly sliced and topped with spicy sauce or salsa verde on crusty bread rolls.

A lampredotto sandwich in Florence typically costs between €5 and €7, depending on the vendor and area. It's a well-liked street food choice that provides a delightful glimpse into Tuscan culinary customs for both locals and visitors.

Top Dining Establishments

Florence's Osteria Di Giovanni

Popular restaurant Osteria di Giovanni is located in the heart of Florence and is well-known for its authentic Tuscan cuisine and welcoming ambiance. This little osteria serves food that emphasizes traditional flavors and seasonal ingredients from nearby markets, combining rustic charm with fine dining.

The restaurant features exposed brick walls, wooden beams, and cozy little seating arrangements that make for a warm and inviting dining space.

Handmade pasta, hearty Tuscan soups, and Florentine steak are just a few of Osteria di Giovanni's signature specialties. Real Tuscan cuisine is captured in every dish that is prepared with care and skill.

The staff at Osteria di Giovanni enjoys giving guests personalized attention and has a sincere desire to present the best Tuscan cuisine. Whether it's a romantic evening or a leisurely brunch, guests can expect a distinctive dining experience infused with local culture.

The ancient center of Florence is home to Osteria di Giovanni, which offers visitors a prime position for seeing the city's cultural highlights either before or after enjoying a delicious dinner of regional specialties.

Mario's Restaurant in Florence

Popular Florence landmark Trattoria Mario is renowned for its authentic Tuscan cuisine and warm atmosphere. Situated in the Mercato Centrale, this straightforward trattoria has been providing traditional cuisine since 1953, gaining popularity among locals and visitors seeking hearty, homemade meals.

With its wooden tables, checkered tablecloths, and walls full of vintage photos and mementos, the trattoria exudes rustic charm and creates a cozy, inviting ambiance.

Traditional Tuscan cuisine is served at Trattoria Mario, where the fresh, in-season ingredients are sourced from nearby markets. Authentic Tuscan hospitality is displayed in the presentation of classic meals like bistecca alla Fiorentina

(Florentine steak), pappardelle al cinghiale (wild boar pasta), and ribollita.

At Trattoria Mario, you'll feel as though you've stepped into a long-standing Florentine institution, where the focus is on delicious, yet straightforward dishes that highlight the region's culinary heritage. Customers can enjoy authentic Tuscan cuisine there in a bustling, vibrant setting, as well as enjoy age-old recipes passed down through the centuries.

Florence's La Giostra

La Giostra is a charming restaurant in Florence's center that is well-known for its delicious Tuscan cuisine and welcoming ambiance. The restaurant, which is owned by the Habsburg-Lorraine dynasty, has cozy dining rooms with calming lighting and antique furniture that give off a lovely, aristocratic vibe.

La Giostra is well known for its traditional Tuscan cooking using products that are procured locally and freshly. The renowned pear ravioli with pecorino and pears and the tender beef filet with green peppercorns are two of the restaurant's signature dishes.

The restaurant is a great choice for a special event or private gathering because of its lovely environment and attentive service. Family crests and antique artwork adorn the walls, contributing to the historical charm of the dining experience.

La Giostra, which is close to the Santa Croce Basilica, invites guests to enjoy classic Tuscan cuisine in an ambiance rich in elegance and history while offering a peaceful respite from Florence's bustling streets.

Florence's Il Latini

In the heart of Florence, Il Latini is a well-known trattoria that is well-known for its authentically Tuscan cuisine and friendly atmosphere. This family-run restaurant, which is part of the Mercato Centrale, has been serving traditional foods since 1976 and draws both locals and tourists with its hearty meals and welcoming atmosphere.

Il Latini has the cozy sense of a Tuscan home, complete with rustic décor, wooden beams, and community tables for a comfortable gathering place. The lively conversations and sound of wine glasses clinking across the room perfectly encapsulate Italian hospitality.

Traditional Tuscan cuisine prepared using ingredients that are sourced locally and freshly is served at Il Latini. Fiorentina steak (Bistecca alla Fiorentina), freshly made pasta dishes like pappardelle with wild boar ragù, and hearty soups like ribollita and pappa al pomodoro are examples of signature cuisine.

Il Latini is renowned for providing friendly, attentive service that makes patrons feel like family and ensures a wonderful meal experience from start to finish. The staff's recommendations and desire to spread the restaurant's culinary legacy show how passionate they are about Tuscan cuisine.

Il Latini is very popular, so bookings are highly recommended, especially during the busiest travel seasons. Getting a table allows patrons to indulge in classic Tuscan flavors in a lively and genuine setting, all while experiencing the restaurant's renowned warmth.

marketplaces for food and specialty stores

Florence, Central Market

The bustling food market known as Mercato Centrale is located in the heart of Florence, close to Santa Maria Novella, the main train station. This historic market, which offers a large selection of fresh fruit, meats, cheeses, and gourmet goods, is a hive of activity for foodies.

The market is teeming with activity and the aroma of freshly prepared food. It offers a varied culinary experience by combining modern eating options with traditional market booths.

Explore the food counters and kiosks at Mercato Centrale, where you can sample traditional Tuscan fare like panini, pasta dishes, fish, pizza, and gelato. There's a gourmet food court on the upper level of the market where you can watch local chefs prepare mouthwatering dishes.

The colorful and authentic flavor of Florentine cuisine can be found in Mercato Centrale, whether you're looking to sample some local specialties, purchase fresh ingredients, or grab a quick dinner.

Simply walk toward Via dell'Ariento from Florence's Santa Maria Novella train station to reach Mercato Centrale. It's an easy 5-minute walk, making it accessible to both locals and guests.

Sant'Ambrogio market in Florence.

In Florence's Sant'Ambrogio neighborhood is a bustling food market called Mercato di Sant'Ambrogio. With its wide assortment of fresh fruit, meats, cheeses, and handcrafted goods, this local market offers visitors a genuine taste of Tuscan cooking customs.

The market exudes a lively and authentic atmosphere, as locals purchase daily essentials. Here, the sights, sounds, and smells of Florence's food culture are brought to life.

A variety of locally produced cheeses and cured meats, as well as seasonal fruits and vegetables, fragrant herbs, and freshly baked bread, are available for visitors to peruse at kiosks. Additionally, merchants are offering traditional Tuscan fare like fresh pasta and porchetta sandwiches.

In addition to its delicious offerings, Mercato di Sant'Ambrogio is a welcoming spot to browse and purchase locally made goods thanks to its stalls selling artisan crafts, housewares, and unusual gifts.

The address of the Mercato di Sant'Ambrogio is Piazza Ghiberti, Florence, 50121, Italy. From the city center, it's a fifteen-minute walk southeast of the Duomo. It is also possible for visitors to use buses that stop nearby, like lines 14 and C2, depending on where they originate in Florence.

A delightful introduction to Florence's culinary heritage and local culture may be had by visiting Mercato di Sant'Ambrogio, where you can also meet passionate vendors who are dedicated to maintaining traditional flavors and savoring fresh, in-season cuisine.

Florence's Cascine Market

On the banks of the Arno River in Florence, there is a thriving outdoor market called the Mercato delle Cascine. This market is popular with locals and visitors searching for authentic Tuscan goods since it offers a lovely assortment of fresh food, clothing, accessories, and handcrafted goods from the area.

The market is lively and bustling, especially on weekends when vendors set up stalls to sell homemade items, aromatic spices, and brilliant fruits and vegetables. It's a bustling hub where buyers can interact with vendors and discover the customs of Florence.

Fresh goods, such as in-season fruits and vegetables bought from nearby farms, are the specialty of Mercato delle Cascine. A variety of cheeses, cured meats, olive oils, and baked goods that showcase the region's culinary diversity are also available for sampling by tourists. The market also offers home goods, accessories, and clothing, serving a wide range of clientele.

Access to Mercato delle Cascine by public transport is easy. Take the tram line T1 (Linea T1) to Scandicci-Villa Costanza from Florence's city center, and get off at the Cascine station. The market is easily accessible on foot from the tram stop, providing a quick and enjoyable shopping excursion along the riverbanks.

The Porcellino market in Florence.

Mercato del Porcellino: Located close to the Loggia del Mercato Nuovo in Florence, this charming market is known for its vibrant atmosphere and unique merchandise. Named for the nearby Porcellino (little pig) bronze fountain, this market is well-liked by locals and tourists alike for its wide array of goods and authentic Tuscan goods.

There are vendors selling leather goods, trinkets, clothing, and locally made goods in this lively market. Amidst the historical splendor of Florence, visitors may browse kiosks brimming with colorful scarves, leather wallets, and handcrafted handicrafts.

Not only does Mercato del Porcellino sell leather goods like wallets, belts, and handbags, but it also offers wines, olive oils, and gourmet delicacies straight from Tuscany. The market's diverse charm is further enhanced with handcrafted jewelry, pottery, and artwork.

Mercato del Porcellino is located between Ponte Vecchio and Piazza della Repubblica in Florence, which is a key location. From the important locations in the historic center, visitors can just stroll there. Several Florence neighborhoods are connected to the city center by buses and trams; from there, it's a short stroll to the market.

A great opportunity to experience Florence's lively market culture, peruse handcrafted items, and take in the colorful atmosphere of the bustling marketplaces is to visit Mercato del Porcellino.

Chapter 8. Best Places to Stay

opulent resorts and hotels

Florence's Four Seasons Hotel

Situated amidst exquisite gardens and housed within a Renaissance castle, Florence's most opulent hotel is the Four Seasons Hotel Firenze. This opulent hotel offers guests an unmatched degree of sophistication and hospitality by fusing historic grandeur with modern comforts.

The hotel features lavish furnishings, marble bathrooms, and spacious rooms and suites with paintings. World-class amenities include an outdoor pool, a spa offering a range of treatments, and fine dining restaurants offering international and Tuscan cuisine.

Situated in the heart of Florence, The Four Seasons provides easy access to well-known sites such as the Duomo and the Uffizi Gallery, enabling guests to fully experience the cultural diversity of the city.

A deluxe accommodation at the Four Seasons Hotel Firenze typically costs around €800 per night, though prices might vary depending on the time of year and kind of room.

Florence's Belmond Villa San Michele

Nestled in the slopes of Fiesole, Belmond Villa San Michele is a luxurious 15th-century former monastery with breathtaking views of Florence's skyline. Situated just a short drive from Florence's historic center, this unique refuge offers a tranquil vacation that combines Renaissance magnificence and contemporary elegance.

The hotel exudes elegance and tranquility, featuring stunning gardens, multi-tiered scenery, and historic buildings that evoke an enduring sense of grandeur. Visitors can relax in the enclosed courtyard or beside the expansive pool while enjoying the tranquility of the Tuscan countryside.

Belmond Villa San Michele offers elegantly furnished rooms and suites with marble bathrooms, antique furnishings, and luxurious facilities. A few apartments provide gardens or private terraces with expansive views of Florence and the Arno Valley.

La Loggia, the hotel's Michelin-starred restaurant, serves delicious Tuscan fare in a beautiful setting with views of the city. Additionally, visitors can eat outside on the restaurant's terrace, which is surrounded by olive and grape trees.

Regular rooms at Belmond Villa San Michele typically cost around €800 per night, while prices might vary depending on the style of accommodation, the time of year, and availability. The hotel is a great choice for discerning travelers seeking an unforgettable stay in Florence because of its lavish amenities, stunning views, and first-rate service.

Cost-effective Substitutes

Florence, Florence, Florence.

In the heart of Florence, Plus Florence is a modern, budget hostel that offers value for money together with comfort and convenience. Key attractions like the Duomo and Santa Maria Novella are easily accessible on foot it, giving it a great place to start exploring the rich history and culture of the city.

The hostel features contemporary décor, light-filled common areas for socializing, and a youthful vibe. The rooftop patio is a great place to unwind after a day of traveling because it offers expansive views of Florence.

In addition, Florence provides a variety of housing options, including private rooms, shared dorms, and dorms exclusively for women. Modern amenities, including comfortable mattresses and lockable storage, are included in every room.

The hotel's amenities include an on-site restaurant and bar, a fitness center, a sauna, and a swimming pool. Laundry facilities, free Wi-Fi, and a 24-hour front desk add to how convenient and comfortable staying here is.

Furthermore, Florence offers very reasonable rates; private rooms start at about €60 per night, while dorm beds start at about €20. Travelers on a tight budget often choose the hostel because of its affordable prices, convenient location, and extensive amenities.

Florence's Hostel Archi Rossi

In the heart of Florence and just a short stroll from the Santa Maria Novella station is the cheerful and welcoming Hostel Archi Rossi, an affordable place to stay. This hostel welcomes both solo travelers and groups looking for an affordable but comfortable stay. It is well-known for its nice atmosphere and excellent services.

The hostel's vibrant and artistic ambiance is enhanced by the artwork and décor, which add to its alluring charm. It features a sizable patio, garden, and common area where guests can relax and socialize.

A range of accommodations is offered by Hostel Archi Rossi, including private rooms with private toilets or shared bathrooms, as well as dorms. Every room is stocked with essentials and is spotless, making for a comfortable stay.

Free breakfast, Wi-Fi, laundry facilities, a fully equipped kitchen, and a fitness center are available to visitors. Also, the hostel offers free walking tours around Florence, which are a fantastic way to discover the city's culture.

Hostel Archi Rossi is an excellent choice for travelers on a tight budget who don't want to forgo location or amenities because rooms there range in price from about €25 per night for a bed in a dorm room to about €60 per night for a single room.

Medici Hotel in Florence

The inexpensive Hotel Medici is situated in the heart of Florence, just a short stroll from the well-known Duomo and other noteworthy landmarks. Because of its central location, it's a great place to start exploring the city's museums, historical sites, and vibrant neighborhoods.

The hotel offers guests the essential amenities in a cozy, friendly environment, all in a warm, minimalistic style. One of the most notable features is the rooftop patio, which offers stunning views of Florence's skyline, including the city's famous dome from Florence Cathedral.

The Hotel Medici offers simple yet functional rooms with modern conveniences like free Wi-Fi and private bathrooms. A few of the lodgings have views of the city, which heightens the appeal.

Regular rooms at Hotel Medici typically start around €50 per night, depending on the time of year and availability. Because of its low price and convenient location, Hotel Medici is an excellent choice for those on a tight budget who want to see Florence without compromising on comfort.

Chapter 9.Perfect Itineraries

Three-Day Schedule for Florence

Day 1: Seeing the Historic Center of Florence.

Morning:

- Piazza del Duomo: Take a morning stroll around Florence's stunning cathedral square. Visit the Santa Maria del Fiore (Duomo) to see the stunning exterior and the renowned dome design by Brunelleschi.

- Scale the Dome: For a sweeping perspective of Florence, ascend the 463 steps to the top of the dome if you're up for the challenge.

Late in the day:

- **Giotto's Campanile:** For an alternative perspective of the city, ascend this bell tower close to the Duomo.

- **San Giovanni Baptistery**: Discover this magnificent octagonal building, renowned for its bronze doors that open to the Gates of Paradise.

Lunch:

- **Mercato Centrale**: Sample regional cuisine by stopping by this bustling market. Savor a leisurely supper at one of the many food sellers offering traditional and fresh cuisine.

In the afternoon:

- **Uffizi Gallery**: Take a day to explore one of the most famous art galleries in the world. Don't miss seeing works of art by Leonardo da Vinci, Michelangelo, and Botticelli.

Evening:

- **Ponte Vecchio**: Stroll across this stunning bridge that is lined with jewelry retailers. As the sun sets, take in the splendor of the Arno River.

- **Dinner in Oltrarno**: Take a traditional trattoria across the river. The cuisine of Florence is renowned in this district.

Day 2: Local Flavors, Gardens, and Art

Morning:

- **Accademia Gallery**: Take in one of the most famous statues in the world, Michelangelo's David, to start your day.

- **San Lorenzo Market**: Shop for local goods and souvenirs at this nearby outdoor market.

Late in the day:

- **Basilica di San Lorenzo**: Discover the magnificent Medici Chapels inside this historic basilica.

Lunch:

The Mercato di Sant'Ambrogio is a neighborhood market that offers delicious lunches featuring a variety of fresh foods and delectable Tuscan specialties.

In the afternoon:

- Pitti Palace and Boboli Gardens: Return over the Arno to explore the magnificent Pitti Palace, home of several museums. Explore the magnificent Boboli Gardens, which are located behind the castle, for a while.

Evening:

- **Piazzale Michelangelo**: For a breathtaking sunset over Florence, take a bus or a stroll to this well-known location. The expansive views are breathtaking.

- **Dinner in San Niccolò**: Have dinner in this charming neighborhood. This neighborhood is widely renowned for its friendly people and vibrant dining scene.

Day 3: Delightful Culinary & Hidden Treasures.

Morning:

- **Santa Croce Basilica**: Begin your day in this magnificent basilica, which is home to the final resting places of numerous well-known Italians, such as Machiavelli, Galileo, and Michelangelo.

Late in the day:

- **Bargello Museum**: Discover the amazing collection of Renaissance sculptures housed in this former prison converted into an art gallery.

Lunch:

- **All'Antico Vinaio**: Grab a famous panini from this well-known sandwich shop and enjoy it al fresco in a charming square in Florence.

In the afternoon:

- **Santa Maria Novella:** Take a tour of this charming cathedral and its world-famous adjoining pharmacy.

- **Officina Profumo-Farmaceutica di Santa Maria Novella:** Explore this historic pharmacy's astounding assortment of antique items.

Evening:

- **Dinner at Il Latini**: This well-known trattoria, famed for its authentic Tuscan cuisine and lively atmosphere, is a terrific way to end your Florence visit.

This three-day tour offers visitors a comprehensive and distinctive understanding of Florence by combining its most well-known sites with its hidden gems and culinary delights.

Seven-Day Road Trip Through Tuscany 7-Day Road Trip Schedule

Day 1: Get to Florence

Morning:

- After arriving in Florence, make sure you check into your lodging.

- Start by touring Florence's Cathedral, or Duomo, then ascend to the summit for a sweeping perspective.

Afternoon:
Visit the Renaissance treasures housed in the Uffizi Gallery.
See the Palazzo Vecchio by strolling over to the Ponte Vecchio.

Evening:
Eat a traditional Tuscan dinner at a trattoria close by.

Day 2: Siena to Florence.

Morning:

- visit the Accademia Gallery to see David by Michelangelo.

- Take a 1.5-hour drive to Siena.

Afternoon:

- check into your Siena lodging.

- See the Siena Cathedral and Piazza del Campo.

Evening:

- Have dinner in the historic neighborhood and try the pici pasta, a delicacy of the area.

Day 3: San Gimignano to Siena.

Morning:

- Admire the vistas from Siena's Torre del Mangia.

- Take a one-hour drive to San Gimignano.

Afternoon:

- Tour the ancient towers of San Gimignano after checking into your lodging.

- Take in the murals in the Collegiate Church.

- Evening: visit a nearby enoteca and enjoy a glass of Vernaccia wine with dinner.

Day 4: Pisa and Volterra to San Gimignano.

Morning:

- Make the 45-minute drive to Volterra.

- Explore the Etruscan Museum and the Roman Theater.

Afternoon:

- Spend the next hour or so traveling to Pisa.

- Take a tour of the Baptistery, Cathedral, and Leaning Tower.

Evening:

- Have dinner after checking into your accommodation in Pisa or a neighboring area.

Day 5: Lucca, Chianti Region, from Pisa

Morning:

- Make the 30-minute drive to Lucca.

- Take a bike rental and tour the city walls.

- See the Piazza dell'Anfiteatro and the Cathedral in Lucca.

Afternoon:
- In the afternoon, spend about 1.5 hours driving to the Chianti region.

- Opt for a rustic agriturismo.

Evening:

- Enjoy dinner and a wine tasting at the agriturismo.

Day 6: Seeing the Chianti

Morning:

- visit a local vineyard for a tour and a wine tasting.

Afternoon:

- Take a tour of the charming Chianti villages of Radda and Greve.

- Go to Greve's Chianti Classico Wine Museum.

Evening:

- try some local delights by dining at a nearby restaurant.

Day 7: Florence to Chianti.

Morning:

- Make the 1.5-hour drive back to Florence.

- Go to Pitti Palace and Boboli Gardens.

Afternoon:

- Take time for a leisurely lunch and some last-minute shopping.

Evening:

- Take a final lunch in Florence or make your way out of the city.

This 7-day road trip through Tuscany is the perfect blend of culinary delights, cultural experiences, and breathtaking drives through some of Italy's most scenic regions.

A Family-Friendly Tuscany & Florence Itinerary

Arrival and Florence's Top Highlights on the First Day.
Morning:

- Get to your family-friendly lodging after arriving in Florence.

- See the Florence Cathedral, Giotto's Campanile, and St. John's Baptistery by starting from the Piazza del Duomo. The children will be enthralled with these historic structures due to their exquisite details and grandeur.

Afternoon:

- See the interactive exhibitions at the Museo Galileo, which feature scientific instruments and discoveries that are perfect for energizing young minds.

- Stop by one of Florence's well-known gelaterias, such as Vivoli or Gelateria dei Neri, for a scoop of gelato.

Evening:

- Take a stroll down the Arno River to Ponte Vecchio, where kids may take in the brightly colored jewelry shops and energetic atmosphere.

- Dinner at the family-friendly Trattoria ZaZa, which serves excellent Tuscan cuisine.

Day 2: Exploring the Parks and Art of Florence

Morning:

- arrive at the Uffizi Gallery early to avoid the crowds. The museum makes art accessible to children by offering family-friendly tours and interpreters. See the outdoor exhibition's fascinating sculptures and Michelangelo's David replica when you visit Piazza della Signoria.

Afternoon:

- Have a picnic, run around in Boboli Gardens, and explore the grottoes and fountains with the kids.

Evening:

- See the stunning architecture of Pitti Palace with a little stroll if you have time.

- Visit Osteria Santo Spirito for dinner, where a variety of dishes are served to suit every palate.

Day 3: Pisa day trip

Morning:

- Travel an hour from Florence to Pisa by train or car.

- Visit the Leaning Tower of Pisa by going to the Piazza dei Miracoli. Take the youngsters up the tower to take in the views.

Afternoon:

- see the Baptistery and Cathedral in Pisa.

- Lunch at the family-friendly Osteria di Culegna in Pisa, which offers classic Tuscan fare.

Evening:

- Take a stroll through Florence's downtown on a return visit.

- Dinner at the neighborhood favorite Trattoria Mario, which is well-known for its hearty fare.

Day 4: Exploring the Tuscan Landscape

Morning:

- Hire a car and visit the Chianti area. Visit a family-friendly winery like as Castello di Verrazzano, which offers vineyard tours and historical insights into winemaking.

Afternoon:

- savor a picnic in the gorgeous countryside with fresh bread, salami, and cheeses from the area.

- Explore the spires and winding passageways of San Gimignano, a medieval settlement that will delight kids.

Evening:

- Go back to Florence for dinner at the well-known Ristorante La Grotta Guelfa, which has a welcoming atmosphere and a wide variety of dishes.

Day 5: The environs of Siena.

Morning:

- take a drive to Siena and start with a visit to the Square del Campo, where kids can gawk at the unusual square in the shape of a shell. Discover the exquisite interiors and distinctive floor mosaics of Siena Cathedral.

Afternoon:

- have lunch at the authentic Sienese restaurant Antica Trattoria Papei. Take a short drive to the nearby medieval village of Monteriggioni, where kids can explore the towers and walls.

Evening:

- Head back to Florence for a farewell dinner at the family-friendly Ristorante La Buchetta Food & Wine Restaurant.

Day 6: Leaving

Morning:

- take your time eating breakfast and engage in some last-minute sightseeing or shopping.

- Leave Florence with a tote full of cherished family recollections of Tuscany.

This family-friendly itinerary combines outdoor pursuits, cultural events, and kid-friendly destinations to make for an enjoyable trip that will be remembered by everyone.

Chapter 10. Activities

Outdoor Recreation and Natural Areas

Trekking across the Alps of Apuan

Some of Italy's most spectacular and varied hiking options can be found in the Apuan Alps, a breathtaking mountain region in northern Tuscany. Adventurers and nature lovers will find the spectacular peaks, profound valleys, and marble quarries of these mountains to be the perfect backdrop.

The scenery and ambiance:
Rich forests, dramatic landscapes, and rugged terrain are what set the Apuan Alps apart. You will encounter a variety of landscapes while hiking in this region, from dense forests and undulating hills to high cliffs and expansive meadows. Crisp, clean air is present, and occasionally the quiet ambiance is broken by the sounds of faraway animals and running streams.

Well-liked trails:

The Monteforato Loop

- Length: around 12 km (7.5 miles).

Moderate in difficulty

Highlights: This trail leads hikers to the magnificent natural arch of Monte Forato, a rock formation including a hole in the middle. Photographers and nature enthusiasts favor the loop because it offers expansive views of the nearby hills and valleys.

According to Vandelli:

- Varying distance; some may require hiking.

It is moderately to extremely difficult.

Highlights: The Via Vandelli is a famous mule trail that winds through some of the most breathtaking sections of the Apuan Alps. It was constructed in the 18th century. The trek offers beautiful views of the Tyrrhenian Sea as it passes by historic villages and lush forests.

Monte Sangro:

- Length: roughly eight kilometers (5 miles).

It is moderately to extremely difficult.

Highlights: With expansive views of the Ligurian coastline and the Carrara marble quarries, the hike to the summit of Monte Sagro is demanding but worthwhile. The stroll goes past rocky outcrops and beautiful fields.

Donna Valley Orto:

- Length: Different routes cover a distance of 5 to 15 kilometers (3 to 9 miles).
Moderate to Easy Difficulty

Highlights: Hikers seeking a less strenuous encounter would love this valley. Here, the trails wind through thick forests, glistening streams, and gorgeous alpine meadows. It's the ideal location for a stroll or a family hike.

Grotta di Vento:

- **Distance**: Cave excursions and quick hikes are feasible.

Moderate to Easy Difficulty

Highlights: Grotta del Vento combines hiking and spelunking activities with guided tours of its amazing cave system. After exploring the intriguing underground formations, hikers can go to nearby walking routes that wind through beautiful woodlands.

How to Prepare and Some Advice:

- **Equipment**: Bring layers of clothing to accommodate changing weather and wear supportive hiking footwear. It's essential to have plenty of water, sunscreen, and a hat.

- **Safety**: Before departing, always check the weather and let someone know your intended route. Certain paths may require some map reading skills and GPS equipment.

- **Honor the environment**: Apuan Alps is a protected region. To preserve the natural beauty for future generations of visitors, abide by the Leave No Trace philosophy.

The Apuan Alps offer hiking enthusiasts an incredible blend of challenge, scenic beauty, and tranquility. These routes will provide you with enduring memories of Tuscany's wild side, regardless of your level of hiking experience or your desire for a peaceful stroll in the outdoors.

Riding A Bicycle Through The Chianti Wine Area

One of the most immersive ways to experience the heart of Tuscany is by cycling through the Chianti wine area. This breathtaking area, with its undulating hills, lush vineyards, and historic towns, is the perfect place for an incredible cycling adventure.

Every turn on the winding roads will present you with breathtaking vistas. The route winds through picturesque olive trees, vineyards, and alleyways lined with cypress trees, creating a scene reminiscent of Tuscany. Bike riders are rewarded with expansive views spanning the area, showcasing the charming farmhouses and uneven patches of farmland beneath the challenging slopes.

You'll pass through charming towns along the way, like Greve in Chianti, Radda in Chianti, and Castellina in Chianti. With cobblestone lanes, old stone houses, and hospitable piazzas where you can unwind and take in the local ambiance, each of these towns has a unique charm. Greve's Triangle Piazza Matteotti, encircled by vintage stores and cafés, is a great spot to unwind.

Without sampling some of Chianti's renowned wines, a visit would be incomplete. Bicycles are welcome for tours and tastings at several of the route's vineyards and wineries. You may take a tour of the vineyards, taste some Chianti Classico with regional fare, and learn about the winemaking process by going to places like Castello di Verrazzano or Badia a Coltibuono. The combination of the wine's rich flavors and the stunning views of the vineyard make for an incredible experience.

The cuisine of the region is well renowned. A common lunch stop for bicyclists is an osteria or trattoria, where dishes are prepared using locally sourced, fresh ingredients. Chianti's cuisine complements the riding experience perfectly, whether it's a hearty bowl of ribollita soup or a simple dinner of spaghetti with wild boar ragù.

You'll pass by historical sites and monuments while biking, which will enhance the experience. Historic abbeys, castles, and cathedrals serve as symbols of the area's rich history. Tuscany's rich past can be glimpsed in the medieval beauty of towns like Monteriggioni, which boasts well-preserved castle walls.

Riding a bicycle in the Chianti wine region is an experience that combines the natural beauty of the area, the flavors of the food and wine, and the rich cultural heritage of Tuscany into one unforgettable sensory encounter. The Chianti region offers an enticing getaway into the heart of Italy, regardless of your level of cycling experience.

Investigate Val d'Orcia.

Discovering the Val d'Orcia entails traveling through one of the most picturesque landscapes in all of Tuscany, with its rolling hills, cypress-lined streets, and charming old villages. The serene beauty and timeless appeal of this southern Tuscan UNESCO World Heritage site enchant visitors.

You will be greeted with a vista of gently sloping hills dotted with vineyards, olive groves, and wheat fields as you journey through the Val d'Orcia. The well-known cypress trees, whether they are standing tall in groups or by themselves, add to the area's gorgeous landscape and make for excellent photo opportunities everywhere you look.

There are many quaint medieval towns in the region, each with a unique personality and significance in history. Known as the "ideal Renaissance city," Pienza boasts well-preserved structures and charming streets. Explore the Palazzo Piccolomini, meander through its charming alleys, and indulge in the local pecorino cheese.

Another gem is Montalcino, which is renowned for its robust Brunello di Montalcino wine. Admire the stunning views of the surroundings, explore the historic fortification, and sample wines from nearby vineyards. San Quirico d'Orcia, with its quaint streets, Romanesque churches, and the magnificent Horti Leonini gardens, is another must-see location.

Not to be overlooked are the natural hot springs in the Val d'Orcia, particularly in the settlement of Bagno Vignoni. There is a large Roman-style hot spring in the middle plaza. A more rustic experience may be had nearby at Bagni San Filippo, which has hot waterfalls outside and limestone formations known as the "White Whale."

Every trip's high point is experiencing the cuisine of the area. Savor traditional Tuscan fare, such as handmade pasta, wild boar, and truffles, at farm-to-table restaurants. The region's extensive viticultural heritage is reflected in the local wines, particularly Brunello and Vino Nobile di Montepulciano.

Val d'Orcia provides outdoor enthusiasts with several opportunities for hiking, cycling, and photography. Via vineyards, forests, and mountain towns, the well-marked trails offer breathtaking views and a close-knit sense of being in nature.

You can enjoy the typical Tuscan way of life when exploring the Val d'Orcia, where every location seems like a painting and every hamlet has a history to tell. Whether you want to experience the local cuisine, unwind in the hot springs, or simply enjoy the peace of the countryside, Val d'Orcia provides an unforgettable trip right in the heart of Tuscany.

Viareggio, with its wide sand beaches and vibrant atmosphere, offers the perfect beach experience along the Tuscan coast. Here's a thorough rundown:

At the beach at Viareggio

With its wide stretches of golden sand kissed by the Tyrrhenian Sea's blue waves, Viareggio beckons. This lively seaside town attracts families and sun worshippers with its perfect blend of peace and beach activities.

Beachgoers of all ages enjoy the warmth of the Mediterranean sun while laughing and the scent of saltwater fills the air. The shoreline is dotted with vibrant umbrellas that provide patches of shade from the harsh sun.

Along the promenade, beach clubs offer lounge chairs and umbrellas in addition to snack bars and seaside cafés serving drinks. While adults enjoy strolls along the water's edge or beach volleyball, children build sandcastles and play games.

Viareggio's promenade, with its stunning Art Nouveau buildings, gelaterias dishing out sweet treats, and shops showcasing coastal fashion, beckons exploration beyond the coastline. This beach paradise is enhanced by the stunning backdrop of pine trees and the Apuan Alps.

Seaside restaurants come alive with the aromas of freshly caught seafood and local specialties as the sun sets. When the sky turns orange and pink, guests can enjoy a sunset dinner while sipping local wines and taking in expansive views of the sea.

Viareggio is a fantastic option for a fantastic beach day in Tuscany because of its alluring natural beauty as well as its vibrant coastal culture.

Trekking in the Tuscan-Emilian Apennines National Park offers visitors the chance to explore rugged landscapes, abundant wildlife, and stunning viewpoints. Known for its pristine environment and breathtaking natural beauty, the park spans the Apennine Mountains, encompassing Tuscany and Emilia-Romagna.

Qualities:

- **Scenic routes**: Several marked routes in the park are suitable for hikers of all skill levels, from easy strolls to challenging hikes. Trails wind through verdant forests, mountain meadows, and mountainside cliffs, offering expansive vistas of peaks and valleys.

- **wildlife**: A wide diversity of animals, such as deer and wild boar, as well as a wide variety of bird species, can be spotted by nature enthusiasts. The park is a hotspot for biodiversity because of the diverse habitats it supports.

- **Historical Sites**: Along the routes, hikers may come across historic sites that shed light on the region's cultural past. Examples of these sites include ancient ruins, medieval castles, and traditional mountain settlements.

- **Activities**: Visitors can go rock climbing, mountain biking, and bird watching in addition to hiking. Visitors can take guided tours or take part in educational programs to learn more about the park's natural heritage and conservation efforts.

Trekking in the Tuscan-Emilian Apennines National Park offers hikers a tranquil escape into the natural world, enabling them to take in the serene surroundings and appreciate the untainted beauty of the rocky terrain of central Italy.

Purchasing and Keeping Assortments

Purchasing mementos in Florence and Tuscany is a delightful experience that blends traditional artistry, cutting-edge design, and regional preferences. A sneak peek at what to expect is as follows:

Florence is renowned for its artisanal workshops, where skilled craftspeople manufacture jewelry, leather goods, ceramics, and other items using traditional techniques. Every piece tells a story about fine craftsmanship and regional traditions.

The leather goods made in Florence are highly sought after; they include coats, belts, and wallets of the highest caliber. Stores such as Scuola del Cuoio, close to Santa Croce, offer handmade goods that showcase excellent craftsmanship.

The vibrant colors and intricate designs of Tuscan ceramics are well-known. See hand-painted plates, tiles, and ornamental items that showcase the artistic tradition of the region by visiting the workshops located in Montelupo Fiorentino.

Famous designers and upscale stores offering clothing, accessories, and shoes can be found in Florence, a city known for its fashion scene. High-end clothes may be found on Via de' Tornabuoni, and unique discoveries can be found at local enterprises.

Food and Wine: The culinary delights of Tuscany provide wonderful keepsakes. Bring home bottles of Chianti wine, truffle products, olive oil from your neighborhood's gardens, and traditional Tuscan pastries like Panforte or Santucci.

For a thrilling shopping experience, go through markets like Mercato Centrale or Mercato di Sant'Ambrogio. Fresh veggies, cheese, cured meats, and handcrafted goods that showcase the area's gastronomic heritage are also available.

Local Markets: There are a lot of locally sourced goods available in Florence's lively markets. Mercato Centrale in particular offers a wide variety of food booths where you can sample specialties from Tuscany and purchase ingredients to prepare authentic Italian meals at home. It's also a great place to acquire freshly baked bread, local cheeses, and homemade pasta.

Tips for Purchasing Souvenirs: Consider craftsmanship and authenticity when you browse for souvenirs in Florence and Tuscany. Seek out items that are representative of the regional way of life, such as ceramics featuring classic designs or handcrafted leather products stamped with the "Genuine Florentine Craftsmanship" emblem.

Shopping etiquette: Talk to the locals, who are often passionate about what they do and happy to share the stories behind the products. In tiny shops and markets, bargaining may be allowed, although it is not frequent in larger institutions.

Purchasing mementos in Florence and Tuscany is not just about purchasing keepsakes; it's an adventure through centuries of artistic and culinary creations. Whether you're shopping for a bottle of Tuscan wine, a piece of the region's rich cultural past, or a handcrafted leather bag, every purchase you make will ensure that your memories of Italy last long after you return home.

Entertainment & Nightlife

With a vibrant nightlife that accommodates a wide range of interests and tastes, Florence and Tuscany offer something for everyone to enjoy after the sun sets. Below is an overview of the area's nightlife and entertainment options:

Florence's nightlife:

Bars & Pubs: Residents and visitors alike congregate in Florence's lively pubs and cozy bars to socialize and unwind throughout the evening. There's a spot for every mood and occasion, from classic wine bars like Enoteca Pitti Gola e Cantina to upscale cocktail lounges like Mayday Club.

Live Music: A wide range of live performances is available for music lovers, including jazz and modern music in cozy bars like Jazz Club Firenze and the vibrant Hard Rock Cafe, as well as classical concerts at locations like Teatro del Maggio Musicale Fiorentino.

Clubs & Dance Venues: Tenax and YAB Disco Club are two clubs and dance venues in Florence that are perfect for anyone looking to dance the night away. DJs play a variety of music from across the world to electronic sounds, creating an exciting atmosphere that lasts till the wee hours of the morning.

Events related to Culture: Florence has several festivals and cultural events all year long, which enhances the city's allure at night. There's usually something fantastic happening in the city after dark, from film screenings and fashion events to art exhibits and theatrical performances.

Tuscany's nightlife:

Wine Bars & Vineyards: Tuscany's beautiful cities and landscapes offer breathtaking nightlife experiences beyond Florence. Local wines are served under the stars at wine bars and vineyards like Castello Banfi in Montalcino and Fattoria San Donato in San Gimignano. These establishments frequently feature live music or special events.

Outdoor Festivals: Tuscany comes alive in the summer months with outdoor celebrations and musical events held in scenic locales. These events, which range from the Pistoia Blues Festival to the Lucca Summer Festival, bring together local culture, art, and music in a festive atmosphere.

Dining & Night Markets: Having dinner in Tuscany at night is a unique experience, as many restaurants serve both traditional and outdoor cuisine. Local agree (food festivals) and night markets, like Florence's Mercato Centrale, offer lively social gatherings where locals can be met and regional specialties can be sampled.

Florence and Tuscany provide a plethora of fascinating experiences that showcase the region's rich cultural past and contemporary flair, whether you prefer live music performances outside or sipping cocktails in upscale bars.

Chapter 11. useful knowledge

Safety & Health

For a stress-free journey to Florence and Tuscany, it is essential to ensure your health and safety. These are some important things to think about.

Wellness:

Healthcare Facilities: The major cities of Tuscany, including Florence, feature state-of-the-art clinics and hospitals that offer top-notch medical care. Call 118 for ambulance assistance in an emergency.

Travel Insurance: It is advised to have travel insurance that will pay for medical costs, including, if necessary, evacuation.

In Italy, pharmacies, or pharmacies, sell both prescription and over-the-counter medications. Seek out pharmacies that have the green cross emblem.

Water: You can usually safely drink tap water in Florence and Tuscany. If preferred, bottled water is typically available.

Security:

In general, Florence and Tuscany are safe travel destinations. Use common sense when handling valuables in public places and stay away from dimly lit or quiet areas after dark.

Transportation Safety: Only hail from authorized taxis or reputable car-rental companies. The public transportation system in Florence is effective and safe.

Natural Hazards: The topography of Tuscany consists of mountains and coasts. Exercise caution and pay attention to any warning signs in the area before swimming or walking.

Respecting customs and dressing modestly when visiting places of worship is known as cultural sensitivity.

Safe travel allows visitors to enjoy all that Florence and Tuscany have to offer in terms of beauty, culture, and cuisine.

helpful connections and data

The following links and resources are useful for travelers to Florence and Tuscany:

Emergency Phone Numbers:

- **Emergency services**: 112. Includes fire, police, and ambulance.

- **Police Carabinieri**: 113.

- **Florence Municipal Police (Polizia Municipale)**: 055 328 31.

- **Fire Brigade**: Vigili del Fuoco: 115

- **Ambulance medical emergency**: 118.

Information for Travelers:
Piazza della Stazione 4, 50123 Florence is the address of the Florence Tourist Information Center.

- **Telephone**: (39) 055 290832. The URL of the website is www.firenzeturismo.it.

- Visit Tuscany's official website, www.visittuscany.com, for tourist information.

Transport:

- The distance between Florence Airport (Amerigo Vespucci Airport) and the city center is about 4 km. www.aeroporto.firenze.it is the website.

- **Public Transportation**: www.ataf.net provides information on Florence's buses and trams.

Representative offices:

- Lungarno Vespucci 38, 50123 Firenze, Italy is the address of the US Embassy in Florence, Italy. Telephone: (39) 055-266-951. theit.usembassy.gov website.

Medical Care:

Florence's hospitals:

- Careggi Hospital, 50134 Florence, Largo Brambilla 3. Telephone: (39) 055 794111.

- Santa Maria Nuova Hospital, 50122 Florence, Piazza Santa Maria Nuova 1. Telephone: (39) 055 69381.

Additional Helpful Details:

- **Coinage**: Euros (EUR)
  Central European Time (CET), UTC+1, is the time zone.

- **Language**: Italian; in tourist regions, English is also widely spoken.

You will find it easier to go around Florence and Tuscany and know that support is there when you need it if you have these connections and information on hand.

Conclusion

As you prepare to visit Florence and Tuscany, I hope the information and perspectives offered have been useful in arranging your trip. From Florence's rich cultural legacy to Tuscany's gorgeous landscapes, this area provides an amazing experience that combines art, history, gastronomy, and natural beauty.

Whether you're meandering through medieval alleyways, eating local foods, or admiring Renaissance masterpieces, may your journey be full of pleasure and discovery. Remember to appreciate the local culture, remain safe, and savor every minute in this breathtaking region of Italy.

Bon journey, and best wishes for an unforgettable time in Florence and Tuscany! Safe travels!

Bonus: Simple Phrases to Help You Interact Like a Local.

An additional section headed "Simple Common Phrases to Help You Interact Like a Local" in your book about Florence and Tuscany serves an important function. It improves the reader's travel experience by giving useful skills for communicating well with natives. These words not only make fundamental interactions easier, such as greeting and asking for directions, but they also show respect for the local culture and language. This supplementary part attempts to bridge cultural divides, build relationships, and improve the entire travel experience by encouraging readers to interact honestly with the community they're visiting..

Below is a list of simple common phrases to help you interact like a local in Florence and Tuscany:

Basic Greetings:

- Hello! - Ciao! (chow)

- Good morning! - Buongiorno! (bwon-jor-no)

- Good afternoon! - Buon pomeriggio! (bwon po-muh-ree-joh)

- Good evening! - Buonasera! (bwon-ah-seh-rah)

- Good night! - Buonanotte! (bwon-ah-noh-teh)

- How are you? - Come stai? (koh-meh stai)

- I'm fine, thank you. - Sto bene, grazie. (stoh beh-neh, grah-tsyeh)

- What's your name? - Come ti chiami? (koh-meh tee kyah-mee)

Asking for Help:

- Excuse me. - Scusa. (skoo-zah)

- Can you help me, please? - Puoi aiutarmi, per favore? (pwah-ee ah-yoo-tar-mee, pair fah-voh-reh)

- Where is...? - Dove si trova...? (doh-veh see troh-vah)

- How do I get to...? - Come si arriva a...? (koh-meh see ah-ree-vah ah)

- I'm lost. - Sono perso/a. (soh-noh pehr-soh/ah)

Ordering Food and Drinks:

- I would like... - Vorrei... (vor-ray)

- A coffee, please. - Un caffè, per favore. (oon kah-fay, pair fah-voh-reh)

- The bill, please. - Il conto, per favore. (eel kohn-toh, pair fah-voh-reh)

- Can I have the menu? - Posso avere il menù? (pohs-soh ah-veh-reh eel meh-noo)

Shopping and Transactions:

- How much does this cost? - Quanto costa questo? (kwahn-toh koh-stah kweh-stoh)

- Do you accept credit cards? - Accettate carte di credito? (ah-chet-tah-teh kahr-teh dee kreh-dee-toh)

- I would like to buy... - Vorrei comprare... (vor-ray kohm-prah-reh)

Expressing Gratitude:

- Thank you! - Grazie! (grah-tsyeh)

- You're welcome. - Prego. (preh-goh)

- It was a pleasure. - È stato un piacere. (eh stah-toh oon pyah-cheh-reh)

- Thank you very much! - Grazie mille! (grah-tsyeh meel-leh)

Apologies and Polite Expressions:

- I'm sorry. - Mi dispiace. (mee dees-pyah-cheh)

- Excuse me (getting attention). - Permesso. (pehr-mehs-soh)

- Please. - Per favore. (pair fah-voh-reh)

Common Courtesies:

- Goodbye. - Arrivederci. (ah-ree-veh-dehr-chee)

- Have a nice day! - Buona giornata! (bwon-ah jor-nah-tah)

- See you later! - A dopo! (ah doh-poh)

Learning these phrases will not only help you navigate daily interactions with locals but also show respect for the Italian language and culture. Practice them before your trip to feel more confident and connected during your stay in Florence and Tuscany.

A Personal Note to My Readers

Dear Readers,

Thank you for choosing This Guide. Your support means the world to me. This book is the result of countless hours spent wandering the charming streets of Florence and exploring the breathtaking landscapes of Tuscany, gathering insights and experiences to share with you. Your journey through these incredible places is my passion, and it has been an honor to craft a guide that can enrich your travels.

Every detail in this book has been meticulously researched and lovingly written to ensure you have the most unforgettable and authentic experience. From historical sites to local cuisine, my goal is to help you discover the true essence of this magnificent region.

Your positive review and feedback are vital to my progress as a travel guide writer. They not only encourage me to continue this journey but also help others find this book and benefit from the information within. Knowing that my efforts, resources, and time have made a difference in your travels is the greatest reward I could ask for.

Please take a moment to leave a review and share your thoughts. Your words can inspire future travelers and support my ongoing mission to create valuable, enriching travel guides.

Thank you for being a part of this journey. Wishing you memorable adventures in Florence and Tuscany.

Warm regards,

Detra R. Cutler

Made in the USA
Columbia, SC
07 November 2024

45922927R00063